In The Thick of Things

A Tale of Undying Hope, Courage and Determination

by
Peter Mwangi

authorHouse®

AuthorHouse™
1663 Liberty Drive, Suite 200
Bloomington, IN 47403
www.authorhouse.com
Phone: 1-800-839-8640

© 2007 Peter Mwangi. All rights reserved.

No part of this book may be reproduced, stored in a retrieval system, or transmitted by any means without the written permission of the author.

First published by AuthorHouse 10/25/2007

ISBN: 978-1-4343-3600-2 (sc)

Printed in the United States of America
Bloomington, Indiana

This book is printed on acid-free paper.

Synopsis

By far the most difficult challenge that I ever undertook is writing this book.

As a relatively recent immigrant black man to North America, life has been rather difficult for me. I have felt victimized by the world around me and have wanted to speak up. I have felt underrated, devalued and subjected to perpetual mental torture. I have been fired from jobs on the most flimsy of grounds and have generally felt ridiculed for my decision to make this place my new home.

While I came to Canada to seek, among other things, economic fulfillment for myself and my family, I have not only failed to achieve that but have now been reduced to being a seeker of the most basic of needs, a situation that I had overcome many years before. I have longed for my life back in Africa and have deeply regretted the decision to have left my motherland. And flipping life to and fro is not as easy as some may callously advise because there are financial costs and uncertainties. In addition, I hate failure or having to live the rest of my life with bitterness and the stigma that I failed and ran away. More importantly, I strongly believe in my ability to bring about the needed positive change for the benefit of my society beginning with myself and hence this book project.

History tells me that we all have the power to improve our society but rarely use this power until we are convinced it is absolutely necessary to use this powerful gift. Because of our fear of potential negative consequences we shy away and permit negative status quo to endure. Going back to Africa would be a bad option and a lack of appreciation of our ability to jointly positively shape our environment when challenged to rise up for the good of humanity. Yes, I know we can do it given the right catalyst. Somebody somewhere has to hurt and suffer though before they agree to seize the opportunity for our mutual good. If I happen to be that person, I think it has not been in vain because I have been appropriately motivated to speak up.

At the same time, I also realize that life can be extremely hard in Africa and have already been through untold suffering in that continent. To accomplish the most basic of needs meant overcoming countless barriers and hence the decision to immigrate when I could in the hope that I was going to be able to leverage what I had in the shortest time possible so that my family and generations after us may not have to tread the same troubled path that our ancestors trod. Hopefully we were to become beacons of hope for those we left behind.

In addition to being on a personal agenda to save myself and my lineage from immediate socio-economic ruin, I have also not ceased to feel a burning urge to share my pain and my views with the rest of the world for many years because I have had this disturbing notion that the rest of the world has worked feverishly to ensure that Africa and her people remained downtrodden. And the Africans themselves, in the midst of pain, agony, ridicule and belittling, have come to believe that they are not good enough and hence the lingering lackluster performance of the continent in myriad fronts.

At the individual level when you believe you are not good enough, you lead the life of a victim and one must make a deliberate decision to refuse to be this. This is what I have done: I have made a decision not to be a victim because I know that when you believe you are a victim, you lose self-confidence and result to the activities of small people who join gangs of crooks and drug traffickers and become substance abusers and addicts. You begin a slow process of dying.

Despite having come to Canada with internationally accredited Masters Education and over fifteen years senior management experience serving global corporations in Banking and Finance, the only jobs that were available to me were those of security guards, bank tellers and other sales related jobs some of which are now no longer available to me. I feel my society has been forcing me to bow out and join the rest of the black men in the alleys and this is my style of shouting a resounding NO! I do not belong there and our society must change. Now! Permitting the status quo to continue unabated and unchallenged is impotent, irresponsible and tantamount to abetting violations of basic human rights and yet we are in Canada, an overtly acclaimed international champion of these values.

My grand parents and my parents lived in a colony in Africa and I in turn subsequently lived under dictatorial political regimes before immigrating to a not particularly welcoming environment. Writing a book in these circumstances has presented its unique challenges. Who is going to be my readership? Will my message capture their attention? Will I be saying anything that they do not already know? I have had fierce internal debates and have queried myself a lot. I have listened to my silent answers to questions such as whether I was just angry and conflicted in my way of thinking and have wondered whether I was going to be on message and relevant. Why do I feel so strongly about my story, I would regularly find myself asking? And the more I have waited, the more passionate the urge to write has become. To add more complexity is the fact that I have to tell my story in English, my third language, which somehow I feel takes away some of the passion with which I would have wanted to communicate. The English tell their stories in English and the Germans in German and the Italians also in their own language. This in itself is a source of anguish for me. Why must I not be able to talk to the world in my own language?! I want to be free to deal with the rest of the world on an equal footing and so long as I have to speak other people's languages, I know someone else has a leg up. Remaining down there would be acceptable if I failed to do a thing or two along the way that other people did. But heck, I have not taken no dime from no one! And yet I have to be where I am!

All said nonetheless, and despite my frustrations, I realize however, that I do not have many alternatives and have to make do with what I have. I also know that life is about making compromises and educating each other in ways that make our lives as comfortable as we possibly can while managing our respective discomforts for no one at the end of day is entirely happy and comfortable for we are all seeking one form of happiness or the other. To this extent I am pacified.

After all the doubts, butterflies, second guessing and agony, I think my immigrant survival instincts have kicked in and same have prevailed.

I have finally made a decision. My story is not necessarily personal. It is universal and must be told. I have decided that my fears must not be permitted to withhold the message. The message itself does not have to cater to any particular group of individuals. My story; my book, does not necessarily have to be successful in my head. I must not commit myself to being the judge, the jury, the prosecution, as well as the defendant, all at the same time. I have resigned to the task of just doing what I must do: To tell my story in the best way possible and let others do the judging and assess its value to them. I hope the reader will enjoy reading the book nonetheless.

Chapter One
Introduction

When I left formal school, I was only two months shy of my nineteenth birthday. Young and innocent as I then was, I had few choices. My life circumstances compelled me to fully accept responsibility for the direction my life was to henceforth take. As far as I can remember, this was the end of a lengthy process of responsibility assumption.

Born in Africa in the 1960s in a family of eight meant that increasingly each one of the kids had responsibility for a significant portion of their daily life from quite an early age. Chores like cleaning after oneself, getting to school on time, completing assignments, buying underwear, cooking, going to hospital, milking cows, slaughtering chicken, showing respect to our seniors and our community were givens. It was however every parent's responsibility to provide a home, to pay school fees, to farm and to provide food as well as to buy school supplies and school uniforms, for these were also needed. By age nineteen, I had developed that feeling of being a guest in a family. I felt like a guest in a family, when you get an inner sense that you were overstaying your welcome the continued kindness of your hosts notwithstanding. At this point in my life, I felt ready, at least psychologically, if not physically, to ungrudgingly accept the fact that I was an adult and fully responsible for all events in my life. I no longer had a genuine need to look up to my parents or to my community. I understood the weight on their shoulders and I wanted to make it lighter for them by stepping down. I did and went job searching.

Looking back, I can today, twenty four years later, still feel relieved when I recall the innocence, sincerity and grace with which I embarked upon the task of building my life. I then did not think of politicians, the government, limitations, obstacles or any of those things that stand in the way to our defined success. What I can recall today are my dreams, my goals and my plans, pure, brave, unadulterated ideas. I can also remember, with satisfaction, the way I went about executing my ideas with confidence and little, if any, self inflicted mental inhibitions. I was relaxed, determined, committed and ready.

It is only with hindsight that I have reflected, with the benefit of experience and comparisons that I have either become pleasantly satisfied with some of the accomplishments or have been frightened by the number of dangerous near misses. But through it all, I have not ceased to feel extremely proud of the resilience with which I have dealt with the ups and downs of my life.

When I ponder and reflect, I have at times become extremely frustrated, angry and bitter with certain people, certain events and certain society arrangements. Nowadays, however, I have increasingly found myself enjoying the grace and relief of forgiving myself and others for actions and inactions that have previously been a source of my frustration, confusion and at times even anger. I now feel confident that I have been able to understand and to excuse some of the behaviors, attitudes and social arrangements that have played out the way they have. I am satisfied that I am not only able to identify the good and the bad in other people but most importantly, that I am also able to rationalize the underlying core factors that lead people to behave the way they do. And this is the crux of the matter: An analysis of why people continue to hurt others, innocently or otherwise. My intention is to castigate and challenge society to wake up and change course. And at the very outset I know this is an extremely complicated and difficult subject. Who would take me seriously? I am aware that some people might even find it ridiculous or pretentious on my part noting that I do not carry the letters PhD or Doctor after or before my name to even imagine that I can have a message that appears to explain the apparent complexities of our world. This is the kind of debate that has played out in my mind for all these years and has staved off any past attempts at proceeding with my book project.

But now that I am ready to be crucified, the other challenge in this complex task is finding an ideal method and a starting point. To make the task manageable while staying on message, I have examined in a rather bold and fearless manner the lives of my family. Going back to 1886, I have exposed and explored the lives of my grandparents, my parents, and myself and our interactions with our respective contemporary societies. Where information has permitted, I have not only described, but have also analyzed and critiqued our way of life in the hope that by so doing I will also effectively be reviewing the lives of others affected by similar circumstances and provide an account of events and behaviors that are not always obvious or easy to explain. If the tone of the book sounds too much Kenya-centric, the intention is to drive the message home from a perspective of knowledge rather than speculation. Since I lived in Kenya for thirty nine years, I am able to draw sensible examples from that environment. The focus of the communication though is intended for a global audience. And the spirit and the intention of the book is individual and community empowerment. It is about the strength from within us to do good for each other as this is the best form of self interest. I strongly believe that together we are capable of discovering a new planet when ours ultimately becomes too small to provide for all of our needs.

I want to be able to review and challenge conventional wisdom including the role of faith, economics, cultural systems, and racial attitudes. I believe I am in a good place to do this because I have been directly affected. As the lawyers say, I think I have a *locus standi*.

Most a times, I have felt saddened by the observation that our world continues to operate in an old fashioned way. I have found it increasingly difficult to find a paradigm shift in thinking from the days of old Europe when the folks of that time found reason to colonize Africa and other parts of the world. As history has it, colonialism came almost immediately or simultaneously with the ending of slave trade. Immediately after colonialism we formed the League of Nations and later the United Nations with its arms the IMF and the World Bank, the global institutions that some of us perceive as having been designed to become tools for the continuation of western hegemony and imperialism with the ultimate objective being to usurp the resources of the weak just like the previous systems had done. It may not matter much that the stated aims of these bodies is to promote global peace and development. Their actions are not matched by the words.

I have felt angry that modern society still appears to continue to operate on some kind of tribal, medieval basis. I have a sense that much of today's social approach and structure appears to mirror the olden days when events and attitudes were influenced by old theories such as the economics of agrarian Europe when statisticians

In The Thick of Things

like Malthus calculated that since the resources of the land appeared to increase at an arithmetic rate while the population was rising geometrically, it was then necessary to have a population cull. I continue to be upset by the sense that despite all the developments and the modern realities of democratic principles, namely the rule of law, the primacy of human life and our joint ability to intelligently and almost infinitely expand the resources of our planet, not much appears to have changed in people's attitudes towards making our world a better place for all. We appear unable or reluctant to perceive our fellow man as useful assets for the overall benefit of all. Like the days of old Europe, we want to cut them down so that we can get ahead. I know I have been cut down and like a brave warrior, I have chosen to go down fighting.

At one time, and I think this was the time when the clamor for multiparty politics had reached fever pitch in Kenya, I wanted to write a book that would have examined life during the era of the ancient Kikuyu monarchy, when queen Wangu wa Makeri, that heroine of a lady, reined before her kingdom was overthrown in a male crafted coup during a pregnancy. I wanted to examine, compare and contrast today's concepts of democracy, the rule of law, the enjoyment of basic freedoms for the people and concepts of a similar nature for I felt our society was not entirely very different from tyrant Wangu wa Makeri's society of that stone age era of tribal queens and kings.

I would then ponder over, and I remember reading somewhere, that democracy is the rule of the people by the people for the people. I would then find myself wondering how it was possible for a kingdom to also be a democracy because the United Kingdom was one of the countries that was pressuring Kenya to democratize. I found myself refusing to accept that it was possible for universal suffrage, the one man one vote arrangement, to effectively operate in a class society, in a monarchy. Who, I would wonder, appoints the monarchy for instance? How would people in such an arrangement be truly happy? What powers would the monarchy have and what would happen if those powers were exceeded? How would the people fire the monarchy? I think what was troubling me that time was not necessarily the fact that Kenyans were desperately seeking democratic freedoms. It was the sense that while people were clamoring so hard for democracy, they also seemed unsure of what exactly they were really looking for. I had this uncomfortable feeling that we were actually playing to the whims of other people that may not have been freer than what we were. I felt there were certain potential complexities buried beneath what people were asking for but few people really understood what those complexities were. My take was that people were behaving like small children agitating for the right to be involved in the setting up of the rules in their home irrespective of what good was to come out of that freedom. Despite all the big haste to get this new arrangement, a lot of the people were still confused as to why it was so necessary that they got that change then.

As I did then, I continue to wonder today whether what Kenyans were doing then is any different from what the western world is doing today. Why would any man in the street be happy that we are contributing troops to Afghanistan and to Iraq? Do the young boys and girls who are joining our troops and giving up their lives truly understand what is going on? Why now? What are we looking for? Who is really calling the shots, and why?

In the case of Kenya, I looked at Uganda to the west of Kenya and the military coups that they had suffered for many years before President Museveni took power from Dictator Idi Amin and president Obote in a military coup in 1986 and the way he stabilized that country. I also compared life in Cuba with such democratic countries like Haiti and I got this impression that it was possible to have good living standards for the people without necessarily having to follow western model democratic arrangements for Haiti was a far cry in comparison to some of the dictatorships.

Then I also saw how South Africa was still receiving positive western press coverage despite the apartheid regime of that time. I felt we had a much deeper need of figuring out exactly what our actual requirements were in running good governments beyond just the people's ability to rotate politicians through parliament. I felt we needed a method of inculcating a winning culture in the attitudes of the people; a different way of thinking in dealing with pressing challenges. I was frustrated that this was not evident. People were talking about *eating*-corruption and other opportunities for short term gain. At the individual level, Kenyans continued to behave as if they were about to immigrate to some other countries. Nobody seemed really concerned with the long term or indeed to have learnt any lessons from how history had brought us to the desperation that we were in.

Since the wave across the globe was that democracy and structural adjustment programs were good, we were all very happy to embrace that global tide. We tossed one parliament after another and liberalized our exchange and price regimes. Notwithstanding, poverty, desperation, humiliation and disdain that we had suffered from the same world that urged us to implement changes to our systems, and which changes we had earnestly embraced, remained intact.

Then I have also been surprised by how endemic conventional norms affect our lives. Where I thought human beings were so intelligent, and sophisticated, I have curiously noticed that people generally only relate on the basis of perceptions rooted down on conventional norms of such things like beauty. I have for instance looked at the dating process and courtship. A boy, having the image of a beautiful girl based on what convention around his home tells him about beauty, would approach a certain girl, mainly from his community and before we knew it we have a new family. At one time, I am also guilty of having associated the Japanese with computers and strategic planning. I also used to associate Indians with business success and the Filipinos with politeness. I know there are still some people out there who associate the British with order and formality. And many Mediterranean communities are perceived as being romantic. When you look keenly you realize how faddish these conventional norms are. Deeper thinking in everything that we do would help a lot in shaping a better universe for us all, but more on this later.

It is indeed conventional knowledge that the continent of Africa is poor, has had civil wars and military coups led by poor, dangerous looking black men. Equally, we know that some Asians are yellow; others are black while others are brown. Some Asians are known to be very poor while others are known to be extremely wealthy. So, convention does not have a carte blanche mandate that clearly defines an Asian, at least on the racial front, and therefore, in my view, they are given a break. They are able to choose where they want to belong. It is not always this straightforward for the blacks and the whites. In any event it is easy, conventionally, when things are either black or white.

When I reason, and at times I have found myself moving it a notch or two further, I have found it quite easy to lick my wounds and to forgive a lot of people who have hurt me many times on account of being an African man. It particularly offends when one realizes that the African has not enslaved, colonized or expropriated the resources of any other nation. Modern democracies and most developed countries cannot claim this innocence, or can they? And yet we find it fashionable to ridicule and disdain the African, mainly, I dare say, for the symptoms of the disease while conveniently preferring not to think too deeply about the causes and the sources of the sickening bugs.

I have notwithstanding been quick and willing to forgive my society because for starters I have wanted to be able to carry on and secondly, I am familiar with what conventional wisdom tells us about the African man: poor, uneducated, ignorant, uncivilized, backward and violent in attitude. In any event we have all witnessed the shootings and crime that happens in black neighborhoods in the western world. Why would the world fall in love with such a crowd? We all love the skin we are in!

When I first witnessed a shooting in Toronto on television, I found it rather interesting and felt somehow insulted when the prime minister of the country was then reported as warning those people who had come to Canada in order to escape violence from wherever they came, not to import crime into Canada. I had just arrived from an African country where the only people who carried guns were the police and a few crooks in large cities. Crime was never associated with any community or group of people and everybody hated crooks and wanted them dealt with in accordance with the laws of that country. My image of the west was extremely positive and hence the bold action of permanently emigrating from my place of birth. I started having the feeling of having been misled. Misled because if I knew then what I know today, I would never have had the courage to leave my home. I also felt encaged because my resources and my path had already been misdirected. Just like that society did to the African slaves several centuries ago. When they freed them, the poor Africans had no culture, a language or even their own names! Where would they go back to? They were lost! I feel lost and I hate this feeling! I feel for them but I also know I have an advantage that they did not have.

I can communicate my pain to the world. I do not need William Wilberforce to tell my story. I also have faith in the world's ability to deal with its problems, at least when they are brought out to the surface.

I have also continued to find it annoying that the western media seems to enjoy portraying black Africa as the land of turmoil, desperation and eternal damnation. I have come to adopt the attitude that whenever there is nothing being reported about a particular African country then it can only mean that there must be a lot of good things happening in that country and hence the media silence. But I realize that my emotions and hurt cannot change anything. I have tried to understand why the whole western society seems to enjoy portraying Africa in this negative way. Should I be blaming the west for their passion of portraying other people in this way or is it the Africans themselves who give others reason to put them down? Is what we see really hatred or scorn and if it is the latter, is it a matter of material class or is such scorn based on skin color and the place of Africa along the equator? I dare not speculate for I know a thousand people will have a thousand answers to this complex issue. As part of telling my story, I hope to contribute my view which necessarily may not be the gospel reality. I expect debate on this one. Indeed, I may even be stoking controversy. I think it is about time that such a debate took place for we have already caused too much damage through our hypocritical silence.

I have also noticed over the years that the same kind of conventionalism that has portrayed the black race in a negative way has also seemed to hold the white folks in an extremely positive light. The world seems to generally portray white people as wealthy, embracers of democracy, better educated and on the main as sitting on the opposite polar end of the black man's life situation. I once had a white boss in Kenya who used to confide in me that

In The Thick of Things

he at times felt rather embarrassed when people in his interactions allowed him to get ahead simply because of the color of his skin. And by the way these were black folks. I have also known people, especially in Kenya, who, when they wanted to start a new business, would seek out the cooperation of some white friends just so that the image of a white face would give credibility to the business in the eyes of their customers. It is not only in Kenya that this positive attitude towards the white race has been played out. It is a matter of public record that a certain king of a certain genre of music in the United States of America, once a very handsome black man and a luminary in his own right, has undergone a lot of plastic surgery. Where we would have had the face of a black man in his late forties, we now have the face of a white woman with the voice of a teenage girl. As unfortunate as this is, the nonsense continues to play out in the minds of so many around the world. Surely if one were white, they would not have much to complain about. Indeed some might even find justification to believe that there was something special about them. I think I cannot blame them.

It does not matter how misleading this conventional wisdom may be. The ordinary person in the street is most unlikely to bother too much to argue against these generalities. Nobody has the time for this kind of social analysis. We are, after all; too busy getting on with our lives, chasing success, whatever our definition of this term is. I believe the foregoing explains why so many African immigrants and refugees are dying daily in their efforts to stow-away to Europe across the rough waters of the Mediterranean Sea. Others somehow just emerge at international airports while others walk across jungles and forests in search of that which is etched in their heads. For we have unquestioningly followed conventional beliefs about success and poverty and our childhood images of what is out there. We have surrendered to being victims and have sacrificed our lives to false hope. This is the same kind of hope that brought me across to these shores. And this is another reason that has made me want to write this book. I have been there, and I know the helplessness of chasing a mirage. I also at one time, before the drive to seek nirvana out there overtook me and I had to leave my home, had the courage and the opportunity of picking up the pieces and taking responsibility for my life and building it up with what I had. I am therefore able to make comparisons and to be rational. I do not need to be here to be successful. I do not have to follow the gravy train in the hope that some grubs will drop along the tracks. It is possible with positive thinking and attitudes for Africa to deal with the rest of the world on her own terms. That requires a change in perspective in the psyche of the African. The Chinese and the Indians have succeeded on their own terms.

The foregoing can be a debate however, in politics, religion or wherever conventional wisdom places the subject. Beyond general observation, I do not claim to have any unique expertise in any of these fields. I must defer to the pundits.

I also realize that a society's value system and culture are deeply ingrained in its people's psyche and any real change to the way we perceive our world is mostly shaped by the journey of life that we have been through. The intention of this introduction is only to lay a foundation for the understanding of the context of the issues dealt with and hopefully, after the book has been read, the reader will somehow be moved from being a consumer of generalities to becoming a more rational, able thinking and a more complete human being.

Chapter Two

My Father's Fate

The January mid-day sun burned the ground hard along the equator and Nyeri in central Kenya was no exception. My feet felt heavy as I dragged them dizzily along the shops' verandah towards the Othaya- Nyeri bus and jitney (called *matatu*) terminus. Suddenly, somebody stopped me. I cannot remember whether it was a man or a woman, young or old, or the color of their skin. But I know it was a good person who worked in a shop. They may have been Asian, European or African. But I know for sure whoever they were; they were good people, who had a shop along the highway on the Eastern part of Nyeri town, near the Provincial general hospital. This person who blocked my way requested me to go back to the shop to take my change and the goods that I had already paid for. I thanked them profusely and complied.

My late father, Isaiah Mwangi was a dignified man. Had he been English, French, American, German, or of some other privileged background, I can visualize him having gone down the annals of history as a great poet, a motivation speaker, a linguist, a counselor, or perhaps a community leader of some kind. He was however, none of these. He went down just a Kikuyu man, some kind of peasant farmer from the village of Kihuri in Othaya Division of Nyeri District in the Central province of the republic of Kenya. I do not think he even thought of himself as a peasant farmer. If you lived in Kihuri you would know that a peasant farmer lived off his patch of land handed down to him from his clan through his father. His wife and children assisted him to till, plant, weed and harvest whatever crops were appropriate and he participated in the local ceremonies in accordance with the pattern of the seasons just as his ancestors had done for several generations before him and when the time came he passed on this rhythm to his offspring.

In the village of Kihuri, like elsewhere in the surrounding villages, men would do the heavy lifting. They would break and till the virgin forest land. They would uproot tree stumps and prepare the ground for the planting of tea bushes, coffee trees and pyrethrum. They would also prepare seedling nurseries and attend the assistant chief's baraza, as well as Kenya Tea Development Authority meetings, education seminars on plant and modern animal husbandry techniques that prepared them for the first time in the art of growing cash crops and productive domestic animals so that they could now replace food crops and traditional animals that they had depended upon for generations before then. A new dawn had arrived and gradually people could see some light at the very far end of the poverty tunnel. My father

In The Thick of Things

participated in some of these activities but really, my grandpa and my step uncles were by far more involved.

You see, Isaiah did not quite fit this general description of a peasant farmer in the village. He was an educated man having passed the common entrance exams at grade four and had moved on to grade five when his father Ezekiel Mwangi Kibii was in Burma where he fought alongside the British as part of the Kenya African Riffles Battalion on an assignment to help win the second world war for the monarchy, the King of England and Wales.

When his father Ezekiel finally came back home, my father was beside himself with excitement. His dad looked strong and able; a decorated soldier with medals of valor, courage and victory: He had fought a good fight, the enemy had been vanquished and the victors came back home with confidence, hope and a positive outlook about life. I have always suspected that my great, great grandmother had some kind of funny relationship with the white people because our great grandmother, who I saw when I was still very young, like her son Ezekiel, my grandfather, who had taken her looks, was extremely light skinned. She was very hairy, and had blonde hair unlike any other villager in Kihuri. We are told grandpa came back home from the war looking happy, confident, and energized like a man who had lived with his people. But I digress.

Young Isaiah met his father after some four long years under these circumstances. He was instantly confident of his situation. He would fulfill his aspiration; to complete his education, find a good job and live his dream of a successful, fulfilled person. At such moments his young mind could not stop mourning his late mother who had died in Mathari hospital just before the war broke out. He could only imagine how it would have been, had Waruguru, his mother, lived to see her second born son go through school, graduate through the series of screening exams, find himself a job, a beautiful young wife and bear for her some wonderful grandchildren. But children cannot be stopped from dreaming and Isaiah had a justifiable basis for his dreams: His father was back and he inspired confidence, ability and hope.

It did not take my father long before he started to doubt the reality of his dreams. He had taken the earliest opportunity to let his father into his confidence. He had explained everything that had happened to him during his father's absence. He had laid out in graphic details how his step mother had mistreated him. He had explained how well his school had progressed and how he had passed the standard four national exams and how the headmaster, Mr. Green Worthington, an elderly white man, whose age must have spared him the war draft, had permitted him to proceed to standard five notwithstanding the fact that the fifty cents school fees and the one shilling government hut tax had not yet been paid. His father appeared to understand and made him promises of a positive resolution of all these things now that he was back. This, unfortunately, is how far it all went. Dad did several odd jobs and lived with relatives from both his late mother's side and his father's side scattered all over Kikuyu land in central Kenya and in the diaspora in the Rift valley until 1958 when he joined the colonial police force at the age of twenty four.

My father's career progressed very well indeed. He initially trained at the police college in Kiganjo, Nyeri, just like all the other police officers in that country. He was subsequently transferred to various trouble spots in the country before ultimately being posted to N-Nite-D, the present day Kabete police station in the western suburbs of the city of Nairobi, where I was born, a third child in a family of eight. My immediate younger brother passed away with pneumonia at the age of one but that is a story for another book.

My father did several in-service training courses. Whenever he had taken a beer, or one too many as we used to say, he was a jolly man. He would occasionally amuse us with demonstrations of his police training skills and the matching drill, language and methods. He would proudly recount how good he was with his studies. He had passed Kiswahili with flying colors, he had also passed several tests on the police code, interrogation techniques, and he was a great marksman: a sharp shooter. He was also a feared judoka and a great hand-to-hand fighter. He was never scared of any crooks, a skill that ultimately cost him his job: He beat up his white boss in 1964 who had called him some racist names. This happened a few days after I was born and this is how my father and his police career parted ways, but once a cop always a cop.

Back in Kihuri, my father prepared the building site for his home; he was going to build a modern house for his family. He was not going to build a circular grass thatched house, like the one they lived in during the emergency period or the kind his father lived in, in the Rift Valley when he worked for white farmers in the white highlands before independence. In any event, he now was well traveled. He had seen the kinds of houses people of class lived in, in the cities he had so-journeyed during his police career. Furthermore, his elder brother James who had had the opportunity to pursue education all the way up to standard eight and was now working in Nairobi as a cook for the Italian Ambassador to Kenya was also in the process of building a different kind of house: A square shaped house that when funds became available would receive an iron sheet roof in replacement of *mugutu* and *ithanji* thatching grass. So this explains the odd shape of the house that I grew up in. There was also a very neat and level compound outside with some very soft exotic kind of grass that made kids from the neighborhood visit our place to play. We used to roll outside and enjoy the soft touch of this unique carpet that only father knew where he had got it from.

The nearest town to Kihuri was Othaya, a good two hours walk when it had not rained. Of course the journey took much longer during the rainy season. This was especially so when one was coming back home from town when you had to walk up the hills. For some reason, all the major towns in central province are to be found down stream; away from the mountains. I think this reduces the cost of building bridges across the many streams and rivers that flow from the Aberdare ranges and from Mount Kenya. No vehicles could make it during the rainy season because they got stuck in the red soft volcanic soils of this place. Othaya is where you found the chief's camp, the police post, the hospital, the shops, transport to other parts of the country and indeed the entire government system. The villagers in Kihuri did not have much connection to this distant place and system though, despite the fact that the entire system was presumably meant to provide for their needs.

Men rolled and chewed tobacco, they smoked marijuana or whatever herbs they found their ancestors indulging in before them. If they desired meat, they slaughtered chicken, goats, sheep and rarely cattle. They would also go out hunting the dick-dick, deer, impala and the mountain buffalo. Large parties could also be organized to hunt the elephant, particularly if these giants ever came out of the forest into people's farms during the rainy season. Men also did the heavy lifting: Tilling the land, axing away ancient camphor, teak and oak trees. Women and children planted, harvested and weeded the crops and plucked the tea bushes. They also went to the rivers to fetch water and to the bush to fetch firewood. Sons got land from their fathers when they became of age, meaning circumcision and marriage or when their fathers died. This is the kind of life my step uncles lived. But my grandfather treated the kids from his first marriage more like his relatives rather than his own children. He chose to pay more attention and nurture the children of his second marriage, just as it happened in all polygamous marriages especially if the first wife was dead, as was the case for my grandmother.

Legend has it that grandma was an extremely strong woman who never took any punches from any bullies of the male kind. Grandpa always used to taut the first born female granddaughters, the children of her sons, by the first wife, who by custom were named after grandma, that he was scared of them because his wife, Waruguru, once put him up in the attic and tortured him with wood smoke all night long. She is also said to have been an extremely beautiful and hardworking woman. Some people claimed that grandpa mourned her for many years.

1939 was a difficult time for a woman to have a baby in the bushes of Africa. When grandma contracted cerebral malaria the only place that she could be taken after prolonged periods of suffering, and I suspect this is the time during which she was throwing grandpa into the attic of their hut, was Mathari Mental Hospital in Nairobi, a one or two weeks walking journey from their home in Othaya. Travel plans aside, the diagnosis and the prognosis were the most interesting. She was said to have been mad and the cure for madness was to be beaten up. So my grandma was whacked down to her unmarked grave at Mathari Mental Hospital in Nairobi.

Unlike their step brothers, my father and his two brothers did not receive much help from their father as they grew up. To get his help they always were taken through an elaborate process of bargaining and negotiating. It took several years before they could get land allocation on where to plant their tea bushes and by this time we were already out of high school and these crops took many years to mature and achieve maximum productivity. Grandpa could also not give them any cash handouts from his own tea proceeds because this was needed to meet the needs of our step uncles some of whom were the same age or younger than ourselves. So, my father and his brothers were not entirely dependent on the resources of the land. They had to look for alternative sources of eking out their livelihood.

As far as I can remember, my father raised the money for paying our school fees, for buying food and for most of our needs from doing such activities as sawing timber in the forest, clearing dense forests in distant places away from home, burning charcoal, trading cattle and bartering tobacco, honey and maize flour with the Masai, the Kalenjin and the Nandis. He traveled and lived in such places as the Rift Valley, Nyahururu, Laikipia and elsewhere. We would periodically travel yonder to be with dad wherever he would be at any particular time. We would help him with chores such as burning charcoal or weeding the crops on the newly cleared fields which after some years he would turn over to their true owners. Many times his pay came in kind in the form of the charcoal he would have prepared and sold and the crops he would have harvested during the years of preparing the land. This is how my education up to the end of grade twelve, the so called "O" levels in the Kenyan parlance was paid for.

Whenever my father was in the village, he was a slightly different man from the other villagers. He used to smoke proper cigarettes that were bought from the shops. Whilst he could consume home brewed beer and he knew how to prepare it, it was not his favorite. He would drink his beers in the proper bars in Othaya and bought meat from the shops if there were no domestic animals to slaughter at home. He never went out hunting and trapping. He was firm and advocated high standards of discipline. He hated illogical arguments and encouraged dignified discourse, linking body language to the spoken and unspoken words. A few people were scared of him. He was too formal for the life in the village. He was too much of a cop though without a formal title or pay. He also had a funny way of imparting order and discipline to his children. It was quite in order in the village those days for boys to wrestle and fist fight. Whenever he caught my brother and me fighting over something, he would give us two sticks and referee the fight. I was two years younger than my brother so I was always scared by this method of settling scores. I would cry the minute my brother hit me and then father would beat me up for crying. If we were beaten by our teachers or by some other boys we were careful about what we reported at home. Father believed the teachers were fair and that was the reason they were teachers in the first place. We did everything possible not to fall outside the regulated school system for we did not know how to explain our role if things went wrong. And yet we also knew that if we had done everything according to book but matters nonetheless went wrong, we could always count on our father to do everything in his power to support our case. We were also not supposed to be beaten up by other boys on our way home. That was never expected. We were supposed to be brave and courageous. We were supposed to act in such ways that we did not make ourselves easy targets for bullies. At the same time we were not supposed to be bullies for we would not have known how to explain our case had any parent reported any form of village infraction to our tough parent. We were required to walk the straight and narrow path from a very early age, thanks to being the children of a former cop in a colonial police force.

Isaiah Mwangi was a man in trouble. Whilst Kenya's economic development had taken off well since the end of the British colonial rule in 1963, his family's financial needs had outpaced his opportunities for meeting those needs. Without a steady regular job or some chunk of land with a cash crop, his ability was severely limited. We

In The Thick of Things

were doing extremely well in school. School fees, however, was a big drain on any family's resources. My sister was the first girl to go to university from Kihuri village. My brother and I were on top of our grades in standard seven and at general high school and we got admitted to National Boarding schools for 'A' levels. Our younger brothers and sister were also in high school. Father could simply not cope with the financial demands on him. I dropped out of school in form five and did odd jobs before finding a nice job with a British bank in Nairobi. My sister got a bouncing baby boy with a married man during her first year at university. My brother failed his 'A' level exams and ultimately found himself training at Kenyatta National Hospital as an Occupational Therapist in 1987.

In addition to working in the bank, I also did evening studies. I married at the age of twenty two and Mary and I were blessed with two sons, Isaiah and Gerald. My sister went on to complete her university education and to become a successful high school teacher and a mother of two girls and two boys. My brother ultimately moved to Searcy in Arkansas in the United States of America and became a successful business man. Our other younger brothers and sister also carved out their specific niches in life. My father, like the majority of people, unfortunately, could not foresee this unfolding turn of events at that time.

I was working on Saturday, December 31st 1988. My department's section head's voice was unusually firm and serious. "Mwangi, this call is yours!" I knew something was not right. Rarely did clerks receive phone calls. The telephone switch board operator would simply take the message if the call had nothing to do with business and under no circumstances would our calls be routed through the section head's line. You see, this was really hallowed ground. Whenever the branch manager, Mr. W. G. Bertnard, a former administrator in colonial Kenya, was in the mood of mingling with staff, his style was to visit the section head's desk. He would either sit on top of the desk, and on whatever the poor guy was working on or alternatively take a seat and place his feet up on top of the desk with the underside of his shoes facing the face of the section head. Then we could overhear him asking what our names were and what our specific duties entailed. We could only overhear, because we could hardly ever look up directly. We worked with awe and fear and in frozen silence. Relief and normalcy would only return when the smell of burning pipe tobacco, that dense smell of unprocessed tobacco smoke, that is supposed to be sweet and classy, at least to those who smoke, was gone. If you have not been in an enclosed room with somebody smoking raw tobacco, I bet you have no clue what it is that I am talking about. But I think the human senses are complex. Once you tell them something is ok, then your whole body really accepts whatever the offending object maybe and you can no longer take offence. I do not remember ever being offended by my manager's smoke or his posture as he discussed office matters with his underlings. In any event, it was also in order for the rest of the office to smoke. So, Bill Bertnard would be smoking his pipe and the rest of us would be busy flagging away at our work, with a few of us also puffing furiously at our Sportsman, Sweet menthol, Embassy king or whatever other legally accepted brand of cigarettes was

In The Thick of Things

in the market. Peace would however return to the pod as soon as that unmistakable gecko brand of pipe smoke drifted away. The manager also wore some unmistakable shoes that made that confident Kho! Kho! Kho! sound as he moved about.

Bill Bertnard was a confident man in his mid sixties who had led a disciplined good life in the African circuit. Rumour had it that he used to be a judge or a very senior magistrate, either in Kenya or in some other colony in Africa or in India. You see some things do not apply to everybody. Bill was British and therefore, did not have to have any Kenyan experience to work as an executive in Kenya. These issues only apply to foreigners when they migrate to developed countries. But when migrants from the first world work in the third world, it is described as transfer of technology, even if they never had any work experience in their places of birth. This however, is another issue.

I once had occasion to visit the manager's office. Chilled to freezing point, I stood there in front of Billy Bertnard, as his white customers would call him. He gave me instructions on some piece of investigation on a customer's account ahead of his meeting with that customer. I went to work immediately promising myself that this was my opportunity to show the kind of stuff that I was made of, but unfortunately when I returned thirty minutes later, the work was no longer needed. The customer had already come and gone. That was the only direct and formal contact I ever had with my branch manager. Formal because my picture album shows one photo that somebody took on a Christmas party where I am seen receiving some kind of present from the manager.

It was at night in some party place although Bill still has his tie and jacket on.

Bill Bertnard got to the office through a special door on the side of the building while the rest of us went in through the main door. His washroom was in his office. He parked his company car, or rather his driver parked his car for him in the second underground parkade of the bank's twenty two floor tower building. Bill would walk up the flight of stairs from the parking bay to a side door of the building before making a right angled turn to the manager's entrance to the bank on the left flank of Stanbank house building on Tom Mboya Street in Nairobi. When it was raining, members of the public would shelter from the rain in the balcony of the bank building, crowding against the manager's entrance. Mr. Bertnard would have his umbrella open and up and he would walk forward just as he would have if there was nobody on his way, thereby making it the public's responsibility to give way for the manager. He would make the same ninety degree turn that he always made to enter the bank. Bill reported to the office at eight sharp in the morning, as if it was a ritual. He went for lunch at twelve thirty in the afternoon and returned at two without fail. He would leave for the day at five on the dot. This was the regular day except on Wednesdays when he went golfing and did not work in the afternoon. He went on vacation twice a year. His holidays would begin on a Friday afternoon and he would leave the office at five on the dot and go directly to the airport. On the first day after vacation, he would report to the office directly from the airport.

In The Thick of Things

During the manager's absence on vacation, Mr. Suleiman Gichima Mangi, the senior assistant branch manager, a bespectacled, not so tall black man, I think about five six, rotund and in his early fifties, would cater for the banking needs of the branch manager's customers. These customers were wealthy, rustic, rather elderly white folk who wore short pants, open sandals and lived in the suburbs of Nairobi in places such as Karen, Muthaiga, and Lang'ata estates, those leafy places in the city where homes were on twenty acre properties. Some Africans who had the rare fortune of owning properties in these places also reared dairy cattle on their compounds. Some of the white neighbors' though were a threat to their livestock because some kept private zoos for their pets that included such wild animals like leopard, cheetah, lion, monkeys and other fancy cats.

These customers were a difficult bunch to deal with for Suleiman, who was a born again Christian on Sundays, owned a tea plantation in his rural home, a thriving general distributorship business in his native city of Thika, and had a reputation for womanizing. How do you begin to pet an Armadillo placed on your desk by one of your customers? Or stop the growls of a Doberman and a German shepherd dog if you have never touched a dog before? No wonder Bill had to deal with a roomful of letters of complaint from his customers upon his return. He would defend "My Senior Assistant Manager" to the hilt and he would make a point of ordering the closure of some accounts where he thought the complaints were too unmerited. This, we all somehow got to know and we loved our Mr. Bertnard for it. So much did some of us adore, respect and fear Mr. Bertnard that even though twenty years have passed since that time, I can still remember his signature, a right aligning curving and flowing "Beeeertnaarrd" signature that covered the whole width of an "A4" size page of a letter.

So, when I was told by Mr. Haron Njugumaa that I had this phone call on his line I knew something was serious. The voice on the other side went something like this, "Mwangi, is it you? Hello, hello, is it Mwangi?" "Yes it is me. Who is it?!" "It is me, Obed Ng'etha, your aunt's husband! Listen Mwangi, your father is very sick. We have just taken him to hospital. Come home quickly!" The phone went dead. I felt a chill run down my spine. I shook. I feared for the worst. For my life of twenty four years I had not seen my father ever being sick. I left the office immediately. I went to my apartment in Kabete and packed whatever I could pack quickly and left for Othaya, a good five hours by Matatu, a jitney that some people are fond of describing as taxi from hell that waits for hours for passengers to board and when all boarded is driven by khat chewing drivers at break neck speed. Highway traffic police would normally be bribed by these drivers and their conductors so that the *matatus* were excused for breaking the speed limit and the Highway Code.

This call came at a critical time in my relationship with my wife Mary. We had disagreed over some triviality and she had taken away our then one and half year old Isaiah with her. I was in the middle of a house move and this was my last day in this apartment. The house move was planned for that Saturday afternoon. I had not yet paid rent for the new place or for the present location and slum-lords were never known for their consideration.

In The Thick of Things

Lease agreements are also rare for low rent properties in Nairobi. So, here I was then, with no contact for my landlord to be or the one whose property I was meant to be leaving and I was just about to embark on another mission whose time frame I had no clue. There were no emails or cell phones in Nairobi in 1988. Few people had land line telephones either, even in the city. These modern gadgets only became available to the majority of the people long after I had left Kenya several years later.

"Mwangi, come on in, son. Let you have a beer", my uncle soothed as soon as I alighted from the *matatu*. "I am so sorry; we have just laid your father in the mortuary, at Nyeri General Hospital". I could not move a step. I could not say a word. I could not think and I was temporarily dazed. I was stung at the core of my heart. The kind of pain that is too much to register. I excused myself. I did not want a beer. I wanted to walk home. I wanted to be left alone, and this is how I was for the next five hours as I slowly walked the ten kilometer journey to my ancestral home in Kihuri. Darkness caught up with me on the way and I listened to the crickets sing and the other sounds of the evening and early night as the end of this last day of 1988 came to a close before the beginning of a new day and a new year in January 1989.

In the last few years grandpa had advanced in age. He claimed to have been born in 1901, although nobody could really verify this claim, in the absence of a birth certificate. But this is neither here nor there. Grandpa never received a pension, a retirement payment or been on any of those payment arrangements that make the payer want to calculate the extent of their obligation. In any event, grandpa was just a Kikuyu man, a tribesman, an African aboriginal.

On the other hand however, grandpa worked on white men's farms, as one of the many farm hands and was paid in kind in the form of grazing rights for up to ten goats at a time in exchange for his labor on the land that once belonged to his ancestors. He had also fought in the Second World War. But then, he was only a volunteer, defending his king and as such there was no payment for him, other than the food and the battle gear that necessity and self interest would have demanded that any employer provide under such circumstances. He learnt many years later that somebody may have used him in a charitable way but such issues were too complicated for grandpa. He would never know where to begin. It would be similar to fighting with principalities. He had converted to the Christian religion and his wife Miriam was a respected elder in the church who occasionally led prayers for the whole church. Didn't the Holy Bible warn us against fighting with principalities and guided us to prayer, the only resource that can bring about healing?

In this defeated, feeble, resigned state of mind, grandpa accepted his fate and parceled out his land to all his fifteen sons, one and one half acres to each one of them. He had done his job and waited upon the Lord to take his soul away to paradise, when the time came, where he would live for ever with the other saints, from all nations, only awakening on Judgment Day.

Within the last few years, my parents had become increasingly restless. Dad had now come back home and no longer felt strong enough at age fifty four to do the tough jobs that he was used to doing before. He felt a need for the comfort and warmth of home. They had now planted some tea bushes and beautified their small patch of land. They zero grazed two dairy cows for milk and a dozen chickens to provide meat and eggs. They had also planted arrow roots and potatoes by the water front on their land, for every piece of Kikuyu land has access to both a source of water and a public transportation route. The land was too small though and they did not have a clear formula on how it would be parceled out to all the five sons, so that each one of them would also have a river and a road front. I was the second born son and I was already married. I had already expressed a desire to put up some kind of small dwelling place of my own on the land but father had postponed our discussion to another day and that was three years before that fateful date.

Every Kenyan man, by custom, has two homes; where he currently lives and where he originally came from. If a family that lived in the city traveled upcountry on a weekend to visit with their parents and you asked them where they had been, they would tell you "home". Home is the ancestral land and it is the responsibility of every father to provide a home for his children. If a married lady disagreed with her husband and they parted ways, custom expected her to return home. It would thereafter be her parent's responsibility to support her until either her husband came for her or she and her husband worked out a permanent divorce. She could also return to her husband's home if it was determined that she was not to blame for the trouble in her home and that it was her husband who was the aggressor. The husband would then have no authority to remove her from that home, despite the fact that it is his own parent's home. So this home business is a serious issue and I know it first hand.

Just when we thought everything was going on very well, our parents were planning and agonizing over our welfare. They made secret arrangements to exchange our Kihuri land for land in Ng'arua, some distant place in the Rift Valley, one of those places where father had cleared the bushes for absentee landlords. Father and mother had reasoned that this land was several sizes larger than the Kihuri land and whilst they were not sure whether any cash crops could thrive, at least they were sure this land was good for the growing of wheat, barley, maize and beef farming. And in any event the land would provide a good solution to their key concern regarding what they were to bequeath to their sons. Daughters were never considered in such matters for they were expected to find husbands. The only obligation felt by the parents towards their daughters was to provide them with an education, perhaps to enhance their chances of finding suitable husbands, and maybe also increase the dowry price that potential husbands would have to pay. This kind of thinking has, fortunately, gradually continued to change following affirmative action, increased self awareness on the part of the girl child, and increased global communication.

While logically the sensible thing to do, in light of their perspectives about life and all that business about inheritance, the reality of being a foreigner and migrating from home did not go down very well with my father. He felt he had struggled for far too long and he was not ready to go out yonder any more. But he also knew he had few options. The land was already exchanged and the last day

In The Thick of Things

for his move was Saturday December 31, 1988. He had in the meantime made arrangements for mother to go ahead to secure school spots for our younger brothers and sister except for my immediate younger brother Mugi, who remained behind with dad because he was in high school. Father's excuse for remaining behind was to arrange for the demolition and transportation of their now relatively new timber house that I had helped them build on their Kihuri property. So he escorted mother and the kids to Othaya, went into the bank and as they always did, shared out the money in accordance with what they had planned. This time though father did not follow through with his side of the commitment. He instead went into the nearest bar and camped there for three days. It is then said that he was seen pushing his bicycle home instead of riding it. He got home late and went to bed immediately. Then at four in the morning, my dad wrote a note to me requesting that I take care of my mother and to settle any debts that he may have accumulated and that he had forgiven his step mother and step brothers for all the issues they had had during his life time. He went out of his bed room and awakened my younger brother for a final goodbye that went something like this "Mugi, my son, I have to leave you now. Do not hassle yourself up. It is already too late. I have taken a bottle of parathion and it is working. I am sorry I must leave." And quietly he retreated to his bedroom. Brother Mugi was twenty. He immediately went out and summoned as much help as he could find and resuscitation efforts began but it was too late.

This far I have lost a younger brother, a father, a grandmother, and a grandfather. Both my father and my grandfather, that I had the chance to meet and come to know when I lived with them, struck me as wonderful and forgiving parents who, even at the end of their lives still had the grace to forgive the world and those that in their way of thinking they had blamed for their fate. I had also prematurely abandoned school even when my academic performance and discipline were beyond reproach. I think I have had good reasons to feel a sense of loss and I have thought long and hard about these things. I have felt a sense of injustice and unfairness has been meted out against me. I have internalized the suffering of my relatives for a long time. I have felt that some force bigger than me has been at play. At one point I blamed the Kenyan politicians. I began to forgive my step grandma and my step uncles. I sought their friendship and their company but suspicions built over many years are not easy to overcome. I participated actively in the Kenyan politics always being careful not to ruffle the wrong feathers. I read the newspapers more actively and analyzed people's words more seriously but about more of this later.

I got home late in the night. The moon was shinning brightly and home felt haunted. It was eerily quiet and there was no sign of life. I did not have the keys to the main house or to my *thingira* (living quarters for young men) and brother Mugi was not at home. It was not difficult though for me to figure out where he would be in such circumstances. I quietly went down to the river, up the first ridge, across my mother's side grandpa's land, down the second ridge, crossed a second stream and in another half hour or so I was tossing in bed at my aunt's place, at Obed Ngetha's home.

In The Thick of Things

As I began my day early on Sunday January 1, 1989, my childhood innocence was gone. I began a new life of challenge and responsibility. I took the first matatu to Othaya and then into Nyeri, to Nyahururu and by about four in the afternoon, there she was! My mother always had a survival instinct. She was trading some wares in the now very new Matuiku flea market in Ng'arua. I did not have the time to find out what it was she was selling. We needed to go home immediately.

We returned to Kihuri the next day. Clan members and some neighbors began streaming in to join in the mourning and in the funeral arrangements that went late into the night for several days. Room and sleeping places were not enough to accommodate all those who would sleep over and as the host, I had no place to lie down. Matters were also a little complicated because the land on which we were living in at this time was no longer ours. The clan had a specific budget for burials and they had no accommodation for transportation costs to distant places.

I was getting impatient and fed up with the lengthy deliberations. I wanted the whole thing done away with. I had not slept for seven days and all this talk and clan courtesies were going on endlessly about small change. I went to the branch of my bank in Nyeri and took an interest free staff loan. As was my clan allocation, I also went to the mortuary to confirm the body was still there and was being properly taken care of, a kind of a Halloween experience for any adult let alone a twenty four year old. It was when on such a mission and from the bank that I went shopping for some sleeping materials and for a suitcase to carry my goods home. I made the purchases, paid, and as they were wrapping the stuff up for me, sleep overtook me. I walked out of the shop and proceeded towards the bus and matatu terminus when somebody noticed my sorry state and followed me all the way so that I could go back to pick up my purchases.

Chapter Three
My Dear Mother, a Woman of Faith

"Wambui, give me some water" her mother weakly requested. Young Wambui frantically searched for a calabash and fetched some water from the large gourd in the corner of this circular cow dung, red ochre plastered oversized hut that they called home. "Here is the water mom. Please drink". "Thank you" a soft voice responded before peacefully closing her beautiful eyes. This is how my mother Rachel Wambui Mwangi accounts for the last moments that she spent with her mother the late Wangari, also known as Wamurigi, for there is no Kikuyu adult who does not have another name.

Wamurigi, the second wife of Kibugu, had suffered for a long time with a disease of the liver, or so they believed. Nobody can really tell exactly what actually ailed my grandmother for there is no account that she was ever taken to hospital. I am not sure also whether there were any hospitals in Nyeri district in 1948 when my grandma died. If there was a hospital, it was certainly out of reach for the majority, for most of the roads, and especially the one that leads to her home in Ihuririo, where my mother was born, was only built in the late 1960s when I was already a small boy. I used this road everyday on my way to school and since it was newly dug up, we would compete in mud skiing on our journey back home from school with my school mates. I have lasting marks on my feet as a result of the many injuries I got in the skiing matches. I also remember the belt whacks I received from my father and the ear pinches I got from my mother as a result of getting home late, all soaked up and bathed in red mud.

My mother's other name was Wahurunjo and she was named after my grandfather's mother. Her father was extremely fond of her and when he was drunk he would brag that he was Kibugu the son of Hurunjo. You see, people in Africa lived, and on the main still do, in rural areas, not in apartment blocks. A man would have separate living quarters from his wife and children and people would normally visit each other out of necessity. Young men would also have their living quarters and the so called family house was mainly the woman's house with her daughters and any uncircumcised boys, derogatorily called *ihii*. When necessity demanded that a man deal with certain issues in his family that would have needed the participation of his community, he would brew some beer and invite the appropriate members of his community for the particular event and it was when under the influence of alcohol that they extolled the virtues of those that they loved. Men would normally sing praises to their mothers, beautiful hard working wives as well as about brave leaders and legendary heroes of their society. They would under such circumstances

In The Thick of Things

only use nicknames, for walls were said to have ears and they did not want evil spirits to recognize and visit those that they loved, as they sung their praises.

Grandpa's fondness for his daughter, however, did not prevent young Wambui, the first born in her mother's house, from bearing the burden of raising her two younger brothers and a sister, left somehow orphaned when their mother died when mom was only fourteen years old. Her step mother had her own thirteen kids, twelve daughters and one son. It did not help matters when in nineteen fifty three, against the advise of their father whose connection with the colonial government did not permit him to support Mau Mau, the freedom resistance movement, all of Wairimu's twelve daughters were killed by a white man's bomb as they secretly delivered food to the fighters in the slopes of the Aberdare forest. Wairimu, who was past child bearing age, became bitter and desperate as she mourned her daughters and became increasingly irritable. My mother had to assume the role of the mother of her brothers and sister and delayed her own marriage until age twenty six. With no school, careers and other considerations that the woman of today has to consider, this was indeed a big sacrifice.

Born in eighteen eighty six, my grandpa was a wealthy and busy man. He owned a few dozen acres of land scattered across several ridges and straddling several streams and rivers. He also owned hundreds head of cattle, sheep and goats. His younger brother, Jeremiah, was a senior chief in the colonial administration. Jeremiah, like his brother, was also an extremely wealthy man. His land covered several hills and valleys and the homes of his sons and grandchildren are dotted on top of several hills. Different people have different accounts of how this family amassed their wealth but this is neither here nor there. Kenya is a capitalist country and several people have acquired or lost several assets over the years.

Legend has it that when my grandpa was a teenager he enjoyed dancing and would attend ceremonial dances wherever they would be, to the chagrin of his mother, my great grandmother. As custom had it then, all the dancers and participants in the ceremonies would be given meat and the leftover food to take it home with them after the ceremonies. My grandpa, late in marrying because of his life liking habits, would usually take these gifts to his mother. One day though he touched a raw nerve and his mother lost it on him. She did what was forbidden; she beat him up with a piece of meat that he had brought home to her. This was meant to be a curse into perpetual poverty for her son. He got the message and immediately left home. He went deep into the Aberdare forest and began his trapping business. He lived alone in the forest trapping animals and collecting their furs and pelts that he would periodically bring out of the forest to barter trade for sheep and goats and this is how he was able to buy and amass all the land and properties that he owned. There is a claim that he actually encountered the legendary ogre when he slept in a cave deep in the mountains.

Grandpa had had a busy day. He had completed setting up the traps just as he had planned the previous night. He had also checked the other traps as he always did. It was just a regular day. His traps had ensnared a few antelopes and he had skinned these and had taken enough meat for his dinner. He had also gathered enough

In The Thick of Things

fruit and forest banana. He had whiled away that evening and the early part of the night just keeping warm with the flickering embers of the fire as he always did at the end of each day. Then he had fallen asleep when the fire was still burning with a low flame. Then sometimes in the wee hours of the night he somehow woke up and from the corner of his eye, below the buffalo hide that he used for a blanket he saw a creature that looked like a man. It was crouching against the fire with its hands just astride above the low flame. Grandpa had seen all kinds of animals and he had even trapped and tried to eat a monkey whose meat he found sour and unpleasant in taste but he had never seen anything like what was now in his room.

This man looking thing had, however, one major difference. It had a very long big toe on either foot. Grandpa gathered courage and abruptly sprung up from below his skinny cover to frighten the stranger. The thing jumped out and ran into the darkness making shrilly screams as it disappeared deep into the woods. He followed the footmarks the following day but gave up when these led him into one of the big rivers in the forest as he was never a great swimmer.

He went back to his usual way of life in the same forest until several years later when his mother Wangui rolled to her death in the mountains as she tried to cross some steep mountain pass on her way to visit some relatives on the other side of the Aberdares. Kibugu then went back home, paid dowry and married his first wife Wairimu and later his second wife Wangari, my grandma.

British rule in Kenya had now become entrenched and the white highlands and other fertile lands especially in central Kenya, where the Kikuyu lived had been taken over. Resistance had begun to build up especially immediately following the end of the Second World War. Kenyatta, Dedan Kimathi and others who had had some kind of close encounter with the British either when fighting enemies together or in classroom in the United Kingdom and elsewhere had realized that white people had the same fears and desires just like them. They started to question the right and the legitimacy of colonialism. The British settlers responded in various aggressive, more direct ways than ever before. Chief among these responses included the splitting up of the people by imposition of selective taxation, support systems for collaborating African families including education scholarships and job opportunities. Brother turned against brother, son against father and the social system that had glued the community fabric together for centuries broke down. Corruption was born. And I think this is also a convenient and easily understood source of what plagues the African society to this day. This is also, I think, an eloquent train of thought; a good account of where the rain started beating us, as nicely explained in the books that I read during my high school days. I read some books by world renowned African writers like professors Ngugi wa Thiong'o, Chinua Achebe, and Francis Imbuga among others. This is also the message I heard the African nationalists tell their people at independence and to this day. If it was not for the white man, the Arabs and the Indians who encroached on our way of life, we are otherwise very good people, a blessed race. But this is a digression for now.

In The Thick of Things

Grandpa's neighbor was Jessie Karanja, a born again Christian and a supporter of the colonial system. Jessie had some education and had amassed significant wealth by way of hundreds of acres of land, cattle and building properties in Othaya town. Jessie had one wife, Ruth Wangari, a committed Christian who was also a mother of several daughters in the same age bracket as my mother.

As was the case those days, it was a woman's responsibility to fetch firewood from the bush. It was also their duty to fetch water and to gather food from the farms. It was also a woman's responsibility to cook and take care of young children. They enlisted the help of their daughters and passed on this rhythm as the girls became of age. I have sensed the western world has a problem with this arrangement and the African man has been portrayed as just a hang about when their women folk did all the chores. African women have also played this card when seeking refugee status in western capitals where the presiding judges are mainly westerners ignorant and uninterested in the African way of life. The truth is that everybody had their specific responsibilities that served a unique need for their society. It was always a man's responsibility to feed his family in less direct ways than cooking, but this is a different story altogether.

The whole community worked together in all kinds of chores while each gender respected and proudly went about the chores allocated to them by their culture, and their environment that did not respect lone rangers. Even if one wanted to live alone, it was realistically difficult. Men, women, girls and boys would visit each other and provide whatever assistance was needed. I can recall when

I was young and responsible for the pasture and feeding of my family's head of cattle, I always had some other boys from the community who worked with me in these chores. We gathered feed together and frightened away the hyenas and leopards so that our goats could feed.

Ruth and her daughters gave tremendous support to my mother as she struggled with her siblings in the absence of her mother. Mom converted to Christianity at an early age, got baptized Rachael and has never looked back. And I think I am able to relate to my mother's situation when I remember how the church, especially the Roman Catholic Church used to distribute gifts to the villagers when I was young. The first time I wore second hand clothes, which have now come to be infamously called *mitumba*, meaning dead people's clothes, was from the Catholic Church in my village. Young Rachael took care of younger brothers and sister well, never sulking or brooding and the bond between her and her father grew even stronger. She was later, several years after these events, when she was already married, to become a positive influence on her own father, when he formally converted to Christianity in the early nineteen seventies.

Grandpa was baptized Stephen which he pronounced as "hiting'eni", the English translation of which is strange hyena. He felt weird, like a strange animal, encaged in a new name when he was almost ninety years old. Not that it mattered anymore. Kenya was independent and over eighty percent of the population was Christian with the Roman Catholic Church leading followed closely by the Anglican church. And we all had new names. But in grandpa we had something to joke and to laugh about

In The Thick of Things

when we sat around kitchen fires, at least when there was still firewood to burn in the now naked forest lands.

Mom never had the opportunity to go to school. It was unheard of for daughters of rich men, such as my grandpa, to go to school. In any event, what would she have been lacking and who would have taken care of her siblings? There was also another good reason that girls were not permitted to go to school. Having not gone to school themselves parents were not quite sure of what was being taught in schools. They feared losing moral control over their daughters. There never used to be single mothers those days. Every child had a father and a mother. It was indeed every man's responsibility to care for his family and his wife assisted him with matters regarding the sexuality of the girl child. If a mother left her husband, it was always expected that the husband would be left with the children. It was also every mother's responsibility to ensure that her daughters did not bring disgrace to their fathers by having unwanted pregnancies and the easy way of doing that was to ensure that the girl child's activities and movements were closely monitored. School would have made them lose that control with the consequent complexities in their social structure. So, my mother's two brothers went to school up to form four and got substantial land inheritance when they were ready to get married. Mom married my father, a police officer and her story became my father's story already covered separately. She continues to wallow and to toil in relative poverty in Ng'arua away from her ancestral homeland.

Education or no education mom has never missed a day to church as far as I can remember. She knows the Bible inside out. Whenever there was an issue with any of her children or her husband, she always knew the perfect verse in the Bible that would address that particular issue.

Now that cell phone technology has finally reached my mother I am able to speak to her from Canada and I did that the other day. When I told her some of the difficulties my family and I were encountering she instantly had a verse in the book of Psalms in the Bible wherein we could find solace.

But mom is not all about the Christian faith. I think she is also an extremely faithful woman to her own Kikuyu culture for the community had myriad rather cunning ways of enforcing compliance. The fear of breaking loose of the established ways may have been engraved into many a young people's minds as if by pure diamond, a hard rock. A case in point pertains to female circumcision. The church then, as today, discouraged this rite of passage that most African tribes used to practice and the Kikuyu fought back with song and dance when it became apparent that some people were getting influenced. Young men would sing lyrics such as *"ningwigurira kimwe, kirigu kia deaconi kiaremwo nikurima kihaicage miariki"*. This translates into "I am going to marry one of these uncircumcised daughters of the deacon. If she cannot weed the crops, at least she can go climbing castor oil trees on the farm." Castor oil trees have thick pith and the branches are brittle and break easily. Nobody climbs a castor oil tree. It is only stupid boys who could have been expected to behave in some of these dubious ways. There were no pants or knickers those days and no girls could have been expected to go climbing any trees let alone castor oil plants. No husband would have stomached the embarrassment of hearing that his wife had been seen on top of trees while working on the shamba. Weeding crops was a special skill that needed a lot of attention and care and that is why it was the preserve of women. Men were expected to plough the bare grounds and to prepare the land for planting and then leave the weeding to the careful hands of their wives. A woman who could not be trusted with this responsibility was a disgrace and attracted few suitors. No mother would have easily stood by as her daughter's life got messed up in this way. So, despite there being a few good Christians, few would have had the courage to completely abandon the critical rituals of their culture. In any event the deacon and his wife had themselves been through these rituals and the white padre never married anybody.

Dowry was another complex issue. No woman could ever get married without formal dowry negotiations and arrangements having being made and such arrangements were never meant to be completed in one sitting. They were meant to linger for many years culminating with the cutting of the *Gichiri*, the shoulder bone of a he goat. I understand my father's dowry arrangements and payments never reached to the final stage of *gichiri* cutting and some installments were still due by the time he took his life.

I was amused the other day to learn that my mother traveled all the way to her ancestral home to complete some dowry payments regarding herself, to her younger brother, who happens to be the oldest son in her father's house and therefore the legitimate dowry receiver in the absence of their father. I think this must be the second or third time this uncle of mine has had to receive the never ending final dowry payment for my mother. I also think I have something to do with it.

I have never quite taken this dowry business too seriously. The last time my uncle and my mother were in my house a few years ago I was just too happy to spread the peace by settling the forever mentioned overdue debt of my late father in the hope that this was going to be the last time such obligation was to be mentioned again. I now realize how wrong I was. I even dare to imagine that my mother could be acting in this interesting way out of enjoyment of the fact that since dowry payments are still being made on her, she remains young and beautiful but this is only a speculation for want of a better rationale. It could also be the result of a fear that some bad omen may befall us her children if she angered her brother. This line of thinking may not be too far fetched. I remember my older brother could not be permitted to circumcise before a young bullock had been given to the same uncle guy so that he could give his blessings. It sounds like ancient Israel, like biblical stories. The only difference is that my mother is a born again Christian. Her life seems to be one of juggling faiths; picking and choosing some aspects of her culture and where convenient to fall back on the teachings of the Bible. And it is hard today to find a Kikuyu family that is not caught up in this mix-up of faiths. I talk about the kikuyu for I was born one and therefore most qualified to talk about them, but I have no doubt this is a universal trend. Our lives demonstrate that most of us are generally mixed up most of the time.

One more interesting and amusing anecdote is that this brother of my mother, for some reason, could not find a girl for a wife either because there were too many girls that vied for his attention probably on account of his potential substantial inheritance or because of some other reason. It is rumored that like a good sister would do those days, mom helped him find a wife. Uncle and his wife went ahead to have at least eight children: I lost count after a while when they became too many and I was busy with my own issues. However, whenever this family has issues, this guy travels to Ng'arua, to my mother's home, and this has actually been the case over the last forty two years, to get his sister to travel yonder to talk to this wild "girl" that she betrothed him. Mom in turn dutifully carries out a sister's responsibilities towards her younger brother in restoring sobriety to his home.

What also beats my reasoning is the fact that despite all the hard work my mother and her children did in support of the economic well being of her brothers, for it was her children who tilled and planted the tea bushes that they harvest today, she seems to enjoy the fact that her brothers are economically much better off than herself. She harbors no grudge or want. She is satisfied that her father gave her nothing and seems to have accepted this short-change with grace. She speaks of her father and her brothers with great love and admiration. I find myself having great difficulties accepting this kind of attitude as sensible, at the risk of being disrespectful to my own mother. I know it is not just my mother who has had to lead this unfortunate life. I know this kind of subjugation happens in different ways all over the world and I think it is, to say the least, dumb that some human beings must accept such short-changes in their lives.

And since we have refused to live outside our mental boxes, to disturb our present zones of comfort, we have not found it necessary to question and to advocate for changes in our lives and in the lives of those we care about. We seem content to continue the course charted out for us by our ancestors and appear to be afraid to disturb the status quo. We all seem to feel inadequate to drive the needed changes in our society. I think as human beings we are called to be a little more than this. Otherwise we live just like animals. Think of the lives of nomadic people in Africa, those people who moved from one place to the other in search of pasture for their animals. If one tried to figure out the major difference between these people and the herds of cattle and sheep that they use for food you will find it difficult to draw a very distinctive line. Granted, the cows would have died if the nomads had not led them to where foliage could be found but once food had been found the mission for both man and beast was the same. Should our lives today, after all these development activity, be just about simplistic animal pursuits? Look at what we are doing in Darfur. Look at what is happening in Iraq and Afghanistan. Who can really tell me that this is not just about survival for the fittest? Why would these wars be any different from the ones the Moors fought with the Anglo-Saxons in the 10th century? We have plugged our ears, and have blocked our senses of justice and fairness so long as our food supply is not threatened. Or maybe we are too scared of evoking the wrath of some ancient gods just like my mother has seemed to be in all these years that she has served the whims of her insensitive relatives.

I have deliberately been extremely hard on my mother. No disrespect is meant. Mothers are the most sacred gifts any child can ever have. We have a saying that if a baby rejects its mother's milk it never survives. We also used to sing during my early childhood days, *kungu baba, kungu maitu na hunyu wanyu mwanderire na thina kungu achiari* meaning praise you dad, praise you mom despite your ashen bodies, you persevered great pains so that I may grow up, praise you my dear parents.

But my mother would have become a very different woman had she not lived through the events of her life. She would not have become the nanny of her siblings when her father was so wealthy. She would not thereafter have had to be burdened with the responsibilities of nurturing some of these siblings even during their adult years, some even into their senior years. Mom, like many millions of other moms out there would not have to carry this yoke.

All my grandpas and my father are long departed and in any event there is no point of stirring up the spirits of the dead.

In these circumstances, I have nobody else to vent my anger on. And mothers are forever forgiving. This one thing I am sure about. When all of you are done condemning me on behalf of my mom, I will go home to my mother, she will hold and hug me because I am named after her father, the late Kibugu, and together we shall cry tears of joy and love. Mom will always forgive me. She is my living goddess.

But deity or no deity is not the point. Let us think together. Mom will recommend certain things to me based on her blinkers because of the journey of life that she has been through. No. Love and emotions while enjoyable must be tempered with common sense. My mother's journey begun on a wrong footing and she became victimized from an early age and for generations thereafter. Her blinkers are fixed and waxed with fear, confusion and events of past generations that men structured so that they may encroach and exploit others for their own benefit.

Peter Mwangi

Where do I begin to explain to my mother that the priest who gave her another name was a money merchant who also dined and wined at the governor's house, the local symbol of colonialism? To gain favors in the eyes of the governor what did the priest say to the administrator. I am quite confident it was about *these natives* and that included my mother. Where do begin also to explain to mom that she shouldn't have been dancing for politicians who at the same time needed her vote as their license to chew up her tax shillings when her children were dropping out of school for lack of supplies and fees? If you were in my situation, I think you would only have one option; to become very angry and frustrated and speak to whoever has ears to listen so that they can change whatever they are able to when they can.

Chapter Four
On the map, Emergency, Kikuyu thugs and an independent Kenya

Kenya is an exceedingly beautiful country. Perhaps I am exaggerating because this is where I was born. Perhaps it is just some kind of middle-age wallowing in nostalgia. But what is a fact is that every morning as I stepped out of my *thingira*, a young man's hut, the first things that I saw were the three snow covered peaks of Mount Kenya in the far distance and now that I live in an apartment block in Toronto, I think that was exceedingly beautiful. For that reason, I feel a desire to provide a small lesson in geography for my readers about this beautiful paradise along the equator. Perhaps I shall also inadvertently be promoting their tourism business. If you travel and spend your tourist dollars on account of my passion for my old motherland, then I think I have somehow given back. The very underlying reason and the core essence of my treatise is man's ability to positively accomplish gains for our earth; our common inheritance.

The republic of Kenya is to be found on the Western shores of the Indian Ocean on the eastern part of Africa between Somalia to the north east, Tanzania to the south, Uganda to the west and Ethiopia and Sudan to the north. The Great Rift Valley cuts through Kenya separating the country into the east and western highlands. The waters that feed Lake Victoria and hence the mighty river Nile, flow from the western highlands of the republic of Kenya. The lake forms a natural boundary between Kenya, Uganda and Tanzania. The famous Mount Kilimanjaro marks the southern boundary between Kenya and Tanzania. Mount Kenya, the second tallest mountain in Africa, silhouettes the central Kenya skyline. This is the first mark of the country that you will notice when you fly in from the north. The minute the aircraft leaves the southern tip of the Sudan and gets into northern Kenya while over-flying Lake Turkana to your left, if it is on a clear morning, you are bound to see the three peaks, Batian at 17, 058 feet, Nelion at 17, 022 feet and Lenana at 16,355 feet. These mountains are named after ancient kings of the world famous Masai warriors, native to the republic of Kenya.

The Masai Mara and the Serengeti national wildlife reserves are world renown for their richness in wildlife diversity and also for a spectacular migration of the wildebeest in the months of August and September when the animal food chain opens up to any observer in a spectacular way. There are several other significant events associated with this country. The Kenya National Museum is associated with Homo erectus, the archeological finds of the first ancestors of man that were discovered by the Leakey family near Lake Turkana in Kenya.

The climate of Kenya varies from tropical along the coast to arid in the interior. The Kenya Highlands comprise one of the most successful agricultural production regions in Africa. Glaciers are found on Mount Kenya, and the country has a unique physiographic structure that supports abundant and varied wildlife of scientific and economic value. Kenya produces the highest quality coffee and tea in the world. The country is also known for its flower farming and is the largest exporter of flowers to the European Union. It has a 25% market share, beating Colombia and Israel which each have about 16%. It is noteworthy that the farmers of these flowers in Kenya are a few politicians and international corporations whose shares are not traded on the Nairobi Stock Exchange, so besides the fame for the country, little income trickles down to the ordinary Kenyan citizen.

Kenya has a population of about thirty two million, a total surface area of five hundred and eighty three thousand square kilometres, slightly less than Alberta, per capita gross domestic product of about two thousand dollars and the literacy rate is about ninety percent. Not the least of all, Kenyan athletes command the world track and field events.

I came to fully appreciate the beauty of this country when I went to Mombasa, for my honeymoon several years ago, and that memory lasted for many years. The topography of the country changes in a dramatic way. At one time you are in the city of Mombasa, with all the white sands and beaches, the deep blue Indian Ocean that is warm all year round and the melting pot of the world with tourists from all of Europe. Arabs, Indians and African traders all speak smooth flowing and enviable Swahili. Here you will also find ancient historic sites and unique architecture. There is, for instance, Fort Jesus, a fortress built by the Portuguese in the thirteenth century, Vasco Da Gama's pillar in Malindi that marks the arrival of the first European to these shores. Then you have the sisal plantations and the cashew nuts and the fishing boats and the shipping lines and the port.

The land rises gradually into the open plains of the Nyika plateau with wild animals including the ostrich, the lions, the elephants and the impala. Then without warning you find yourself traversing through Masai and Kamba land - each place with its unique and proud history.

Before you know it you find yourself in the ever cool Nairobi where you find another melting pot with people from around the world. You might either decide to stay or head out west to wheat country in the Great Rift Valley before getting into western Kenya where you find Lake Victoria, the Aberdare ranges, the Mau ranges, and the western highlands full of tea and sugarcane plantations. One could also head out North towards Mount Kenya through the coffee and the tea plantations of Nyeri and Meru and the grasslands and wheat country in Nanyuki and the animal reserves in the far North towards Ethiopia and the Sudan.

Because of these endowments, Kenyans have remained relatively well off economically when compared to most other African countries. The country has also enjoyed relative peace since independence and has cultivated positive relationships with the rest of the world. But one

In The Thick of Things

of the major sources of national income is tourism. And tourists have their various tastes that a country that thrives on their custom may find difficult to meet or worse than that find itself sacrificing the interests of its own people in order that it does not lose tourist dollars. Kenya was a British colony until 1963 when the country gained her independence and European tourists, particularly the British, form a significant source of tourist business.

To gain the custom of the tourists, you will increasingly find Kenyans struggling hard to speak English the way the English speak it, or some even practicing outdated British customs. A good example is the old English infatuation with the manner of how to hold a knife and fork. Some Kenyans will also want to be seen to spite their own cuisine in preference for egg and bacon for breakfast. The traditional staple is maize meal cake eaten with beef stew, milk or fish. It is unlikely that a guest to a Kenyan family would be served this staple on the first day. Most families will go out of their way to give their guests something 'better'. Some of these mannerisms can provide interesting sitcoms and many a times make Kenyans appear awkward and lacking in confidence. One politician, the late Jaramogi Oginga Odinga, was so pissed off that he announced that it was not yet Uhuru. He was frustrated that despite the country having secured her independence, people still behaved in extremely subservient ways towards foreigners, especially if these foreigners happened to be white and spoke English. I think the English must have been extremely good in the way they went about colonizing other people. They did it really good and this has lingered on for generations, for better or for worse.

Peter Mwangi

As a child of freedom, for I was born on the dawn of independence in 1963, it is difficult for me to tell the story of my life without intricately entangling it up with that country's political landscape, for this is how it always was; tangled up in the country's body politic. In fact this is not unique to me. My age-mate Mr. Uhuru Kenyatta, the leader of the official opposition in that country, is named after independence, *uhuru* meaning independence and *Kenyatta,* meaning from Kenya. This reflects the pride with which that nation felt for being able to govern itself, or so it may appear on the face of it.

In the thirty nine years that I lived in that country we were ruled by two leaders; one for fifteen years and the other for twenty four years. Jomo Kenyatta was the first one, and he died in office. I was still too young to understand or to care about his politics for he came to power on the year that I was born and passed on a year before I went to senior high school. His legacy and portraits linger on and there is no way that one can talk about Kenya without talking about Jomo Kenyatta. I think it would be like talking about British prime ministers without talking about Winston Churchill.

For fifteen years, Kenya was Jomo Kenyatta and Jomo Kenyatta was Kenya. There are some enduring myths and lessons and customs built around this powerful man of yesteryears in that country. To this day, if I spotted a black cat crossing the road when driving, I am forced to drive very carefully thereafter for there is a myth in Kenya that says Jomo Kenyatta's motorcade would never proceed on a journey if they ever spotted a black cat crossing the road ahead. Kenyatta acquired and amassed significant tracts of land and other resources. He governed and behaved like a mighty lord over his people, their demigod. His word was law and he operated above the law. It was common understanding that if he wanted a certain individual to become a member of parliament, he had no hesitation in announcing for all to hear that his vote and Ngina's vote were sufficient to get that individual to parliament. And so it would happen. Ngina happened to be his youngest wife, who was generally understood to have been bequeathed to Kenyatta by her family, an important family in their own right, as a betrothal for a bond of friendship between the two families. Kenyatta had other wives including some that he had married many years before he traveled to study in London as well as the one he met during his period of study. I think the family troubles that beset small men never affect all men, just like they say in *Animal Farm* that some animals are more equal than others.

But let the truth be told, I think Kenyatta was also a very able leader. There were no civil wars in the country. One exception was north eastern Kenya where the Somalis wanted a separate republic for they felt that they were aligned more with the clans of Somaliland and Nairobi was not likely to accommodate their unique needs. Kenyatta's government unleashed terror to contain them and there was a separate policy for "NFD", the Northern Frontier Districts. And as if to send an even stronger message, development activities in this part of the country were never initiated. The Kenyan Somali community lagged behind the rest of the country in many ways and their hostility towards their government justifiably continued to grow. Whereas most Kenyans are within walking distance of a high school or a dispensary, the Somalis are still dependent on the charity of international non-profit organizations to provide for the basics of life. The rest of Kenya moved on in a spectacular way on relative terms.

Several economic opportunities were created, and the whole government system was properly energized. Kenyatta rarely contradicted his ministers. The cooperative movement was started through the efforts of his government and a respectable school system, where none previously existed, was established. The Central Bank, government ministries, countless hospitals and a respectable web of government infrastructure was put in place.

Beyond these local development activities, Kenyatta also realized at the very beginning that Kenyans were too unprepared for a new government and he worked closely with developed countries for technology transfer. Despite the fierce resistance against the rule of the British, Jomo Kenyatta still gave the Kenyan British the freedom of making a choice to either stay or leave and many have remained post-independence with their farms and other assets intact. I think there were just too many expectations that an old man of his age, for he took power when he was 72, could fulfill in his active years of service in an environment that was not entirely ready for all the challenges of running a government. And his society looked up to him to rule with authority, charisma and ability now that he had taken over from the mighty British. The British tentacles were well woven and unfortunately, not in his favor. I do not think he would have survived had he not threatened the fear of god in the minds of his people. And to demonstrate that people's

In The Thick of Things

fear had a reasonable basis, Kenyatta was accused of being responsible for a number of political assassinations, namely those of Hon. Tom Mboya, Kung'u Kurumba and Hon. Josiah Mwangi Kariuki. Some people felt it was not possible to mess up with Kenyatta and still expect to live. People felt that he was in some way able to get you. You would then either disappear into the hills of the Ngong forest near Nairobi, a sniper's bullet could take you out as you walked in downtown Nairobi, or you simply vanished. Investigations would be conducted for years without any arrests or closure. Those who loved their lives kept a respectable distance from Jomo Kenyatta the man.

Jomo Kenyatta was also a well rounded person. Long before independence, he had worked as a clerk for the city of Nairobi as a water meter reader. Born Kamau, the son of Ngengi Muigai, he at the age of 46 applied and earned a scholarship to study anthropology in London, England where he spent 16 years. He spoke with authority and was a great orator in Kikuyu, Kiswahili and English. He was a big man with a square jaw, wore rugged leather jackets and he deeply understood and practiced the rituals of his culture. He was indeed nobody's push over. During his days in detention between 1952 and 1960 Jomo Kenyatta wrote several books. He is also the author of the a best selling novel *Facing Mount Kenya,* because from the window of his jail room in Kapenguria, he was always facing Mount Kenya and this kept his dream of one day taking the responsibility of leading his nation and his people alive.

Jomo Kenyatta was also a fair man, at least if you did not threaten or belittle his authority. He appointed ministers from all over the country and from different communities. His task was however made difficult by the fact that he was the first president, his people had not had previous experience with governing themselves and therefore their basis for assessing his performance was not always rational. If a minister for instance was ever fired from a job, it was perceived not as a personal loss, but rather as a tribal loss, and politicians have played this card to their advantage for decades henceforth. When Jaramogi Oginga Odinga, the then vice president, broke ranks with Kenyatta to form a separate political party in 1969, almost the entire Luo community broke ranks not just with Kenyatta but also with Kenyatta's community- the Kikuyu. These animosities have been played out to this day, reducing well traveled university professors to nothing more than tribal chiefs.

The other big man who lorded it over my country during my adolescence and a bigger chunk of my adult life was Daniel Toroitich Arap Moi, otherwise infamously nicknamed Uncle Dan or *Nyayo*, meaning foot prints. Daniel had been the timid vice president under President Kenyatta in the seventies. He served Jomo Kenyatta with so much reverence and dedication that even in Kenyatta's death and when uncle Dan became the big man, he dared not give any signals that he was about to introduce any sweeping changes of his own. This was to become a big surprise to many people. Some people initially thought he was just a passing cloud and many made no secret about this. This was a complete misunderstanding of who Dan really was. But when compared to Mzee Kenyatta's demeanor, and political clout, he was indeed a very small

In The Thick of Things

man. I think by many accounts most people would have indeed been very small compared to Jomo Kenyatta.

All said President Moi was anything but a passing cloud. At the very outset, he promised the country that he would lead strictly on the basis of the footsteps of his mentor and able leader the late president Kenyatta. Or so the people understood him to be saying for Africans have a figurative way of speaking. What Moi actually meant was that since Kenyatta had spent the time pushing the agenda of his own tribe, the Kikuyu, Moi was also to equally use the authority of his presidency in propagating the agenda of his own tribesmen, the Kalenjin, and hence the Nyayo mantra. And everywhere he went everybody shouted *Nyayo!, Nyayo!, Nyayo!*. By default the people of Kenya gave Moi the right to use and plunder their tax shillings to extend nepotism to his tribesmen at the expense of their country.

If you were visiting a particular town and the president paid a visit to that town, you would hear loud speakers announcing his arrival with repeated shouts of *Nyayo! Nyayo! Karibu! Karibu! Karibu Mtukufu Rais Wetu! Karibu! Karibu baba wa Taifa! Karibu! Karibu! Karibu!* Meaning welcome! Welcome! Welcome! Welcome our almighty president! Welcome! Welcome father of the nation! Welcome! Welcome! Welcome! There could never have been the vaguest shadow of doubt that the particular town or hamlet had any hesitations concerning their love for their almighty president. It is strange and interesting how fate handles life. Moi is now just an old man in retirement in Kenya.

Our new lord and king *Nyayo* was also internationally very well connected. It is during his rein that the queen of England came to visit Kenya. Other world leaders also came over to support his reign and his power became even more entrenched. Moi also introduced a new philosophy of peace, love and unity. Musicians composed songs in his honor and poets composed poetry with lyrics that recognized the great leader. His motto and philosophy of *peace, love and unity* became an examinable subject that was taught in schools alongside the Nyayo national anthem, separate from the regular national anthem. He also introduced a Nyayo day, which commemorated the day he ascended into power, 10th October 1978. Monuments were built all over the country glorifying his leadership and I think there were more Moi high schools, Moi universities, and Moi hospitals than there were qualified professionals to run those institutions.

Poverty and political persecutions became a regular feature and many Kenyans left that country. Government appointments became the preserve of only a few. All government ministries, the judiciary, the military, the police force and crown corporations were staffed with the same families. There was no service whatsoever and people spoke one tribal language in the offices in a nation of at least forty two ethnic communities. The country has only two recognized national languages that are taught and examined in schools in order to put some order in light of all these different communities and dialects. But in the Nyayo era the whole government became a sham, a chieftain staffed with tribal warriors and their girlfriends. I did not know anybody in my community who worked for the government and those who used to work there before the nyayo days were either overseas or in jail. I never imagined that it was ever possible for me to work for a government to the extent that even when I came to Canada, I did not apply for any government jobs in four years. Government belonged to other people, besides me. I did not know how to speak government language. Mine was to pay taxes and to sustain those in government. Since my pay was good in the private sector for many years it really never bothered me too much, at least financially but I always had a big problem intellectually. It also bothered me that we were plundering so much of the resources of our nation and shaming ourselves so much on the international arena. I always felt curtailed and disabled from being able to effectively play my role in my society.

Moi also to a good measure followed in Kenyatta's footsteps and did several deeds worthy of praise. It was during his rein that six national public universities were opened up. Several hospital wards and schools were also started and Kenya never failed to pay her international debts. Moi was also an ambitious president for his country. He began several projects most of which later turned into white elephants and some of these were conduits for mega corruption. Some people became exceedingly wealthy at the expense of the poor masses. The press had it that certain high ranking individuals owned farms in the prairies of North America. During times of grain shortage, administrative measures would be introduced permitting importers to bring in wheat from foreign countries without paying the usual customs duty. As soon as the shiploads of the connected individual's wheat landed, the administrative exceptions would be lifted thereby making it prohibitively expensive for the unconnected investors.

Peter Mwangi

While some people were being pauperized, others became overnight millionaires. The private sector supported and abetted Moi's style. I worked for an international bank that could not transfer certain people to certain less lucrative parts of the country and which appointed into its board of directors some of Moi's henchmen. The madness was spread all over the country like a dangerous cancer.

Even the school system that has prefects, going all the way back to kindergarten, found itself looking for Kalenjin prefects especially in the larger towns where there is wider multi-ethnicity. University entry points were realigned and lecturers and professors were appointed on the basis of tribal fit.

The police force had many tentacles including the special branch that was not only made up of the regular members of the force, but also included several private cells that pervaded the entire landscape. Nobody spoke without looking behind their ears. Why? Because Moi had also cracked his whip. If you were Kikuyu, you were forever a suspect. I think I see the same kind of thing regarding Muslims especially in the United States. You were guilty by virtue of your name. The police would on a regular basis arrest young boys, as young as fifteen or seventeen, and accuse them of carrying out plots to overthrow the government. It did not matter that some of these youngsters did not even know how guns looked like let alone use them, because only the police are legally permitted to carry guns in that country. Even the police are required to return the guns to the government armory whenever not on police duty. I have never known a friend or a relative who ever carried a gun and have

In The Thick of Things

only seen these weapons from a distance. It is the same thing for the majority of Kenyans. This did not stop the government press from concocting conspiracy theories about how certain individuals who are now in the current government, such as Hon. Koigi wa Wamwere, were then planning with the help of their teenage relatives to overthrow Moi. At one time there was a huge story that Koigi and others had raided a small police station in order to steal guns for the purpose of overthrowing Moi. We were treated from one information circus into another as this big man extended his political hegemony.

Political assassinations also happened during Moi's reign and the death of Hon Robert Ouko, the then minister of Foreign Affairs and international cooperation was attributed to Moi and his underlings. The lives of several innocent people were ruined in jail.

During these twenty four years of Arap Moi, by the way Arap stands for son of, ending December 2002, everybody knew every Sunday where President Arap Moi had been to church, and how much he had contributed to the church kitty and what he had said to the worshippers. He could also appoint ministers after the service or announce some major policy changes at a time of his choosing. The president was able to behave in this paternalistic way despite the fact that the country had had democratic elections every five years since her independence.

Moi also had a unique personality. He reported to his office at seven in the morning daily for twenty four years and never went on vacation other than short overseas business trips. He had a quick wit and was a great comedian. He had an extremely kind personality to those near him and maintained great composure even when extremely angry. And he was for ever humble in his manner of speech and demeanor to the extent that despite all the harm that was attributed to his regime, a lot of people including those in the diplomatic corps still found it difficult to pin it to Moi as a person. They found it easy to excuse him as dull and actually argue that other people were the de facto presidents. People were always wondering how this humble looking born again Christian who cracked jokes all the time be at the same time responsible for so much evil.

So religion and the Christian faith have been very close to my heart because I have had all this time to observe and to think about it. Politics and religion were the soap operas on Kenyan television. And of course, the various economic development initiatives, social changes and programs also affected my life in several fundamental ways. The chronology of events leading to Jomo Kenyatta and subsequently to Moi started with the colonial legacy.

On the main, relationships between the British settlers and the Africans had remained cordial, despite the master servant dimension that imperialism and colonization entailed. Subterranean discomforts would periodically simmer but in general everybody was otherwise settled down and getting on with their life. Matters however, gradually developed to a head in the years between 1927 and 1952. During these years, there came Harry Thuku with his Kenya African Union in 1927 and then there is the story about Jomo Kenyatta going to school in England until 1946. Then the crunch came in 1952

In The Thick of Things

when a state of emergency was declared after some gangs that were later identified as *Mau Mau* murdered several white farmers.

The colonial government decided it was about time and like Nazi Germany or Apartheid South Africa gradually adopted tougher measures to deter the rising resistance movement that had now come to be identified with the Kikuyu people. This was an industrious farming community that had established a web of relationships with the British people in Kenya. Their leadership and involvement in the uprising was particularly angering to the British settlers because these were among the largest group of local people that had benefited most from the colonization of Kenya. They had found jobs in the coffee and tea plantations, in homes with older men working as cooks, herdsmen and in other sundry jobs. Younger men found work as office messengers, drivers, and race-horse jockeys. The entire system was progressing on well, albeit at quite a slow pace towards ,among other things, giving these people an education that would have prepared them for better jobs. When one visualizes the mindset of an ordinary white farmer in Kenya in 1952, one might find it sensible that the poor guy may have felt a legitimate basis to feel cheated. He had done everything to appease these people and now here they were baying for his guts. *Murderous brutes!* he may have found himself cursing.

Between the time of the scramble for Africa in 1886, and 1952, the British had made significant inroads in Kenya. The Old East African Trading Company had completed the Kenya-Uganda railway line. The port of Mombasa on the Indian Ocean, to the East, and the Port of Kisumu on Lake Victoria to the west had been completed and several railway towns had sprung up. King George Hospital, the present day Kenyatta National Hospital, had been built. Another branch of the railway line to Nanyuki on the foothills of Mount Kenya to the north had opened up another productive part of the country. Trading towns such as Fort Hall, the present day Murang'a, and Thika had opened up. The city of Nairobi opened up in 1905 and financial institutions such as Standard Chartered Bank that opened its first office in 1910 were in place. There was so much on the go and most white settlers to Kenya had no plans of ever going anywhere else. They had invested whatever they could and they were at home. In fact educational institutions such as Nairobi School, Lenana high school, and Mang'u high school were already in place to provide for the educational needs of their children and a few African kids in preparation for further education in the United Kingdom.

The church had, initially through the Africa Inland Mission, established itself in Rabai, through the work of missionaries such as the late Ludwig Krapf and John Rebman. It later quickly spread to Mombasa, Nairobi and across the whole country with more denominations and sects introducing their style and converting believers. There was a large following of the Roman Catholic Church, the Anglican Church and the Pentecostal church. The Africans also planted their own churches such as the African Independent Pentecostal Church and the Akorino sect that among other things permitted the Africans to convert to Christianity while still maintaining their traditions such as female circumcision.

In The Thick of Things

Then all of a sudden, like in a bad dream, these natives begin their resistance movements. Whilst not caught by a complete surprise, the degree of damage, cunning and planning seemed to confound most people. What do these people want, people would ask each other? Why are these *animals* never satisfied? We have provided them with everything and god knows they would still be walking naked had the settlers never came over. Of course a few wise people understood that the natives had not asked for the clothes that they were now wearing in the first place.

There is a Swahili saying that *"Nyani halioni kundu lake"*. The English translation of this is that a monkey does not see its bare butt but it only laughs at the ugliness of the butts of other monkeys. It was easy for the white settlers to count their losses and most of them felt quite justified in doing so. Just for the sake of debate assume it had been your grand parent who had immigrated to some unknown place, and as an immigrant myself, I think I can very well relate to this. Now you find yourself , the second or third generation after, wondering what business you have paying for the sins of your father if it ever happened that some so called natives did not feel that they were being given equal rights. It may not matter much that some native guys are catering to your every whim and that they felt like they were less privileged than yourself. It is also appropriate to put into perspective the fact that even at that time, Great Britain was still a capitalist society, and we all know the beast that capitalism is. The winner takes it all and there are no free lunches or money machines. Everybody gets what they work for and if they are lazy or naïve and leave their barn door open, the horses bolt away and they have only got themselves to blame. In this manner, tempers flared and the government's grip tightened. The whip cracked. And the natives got it rough. I know a few of my relatives who got a taste of this and it was not very entertaining. I think the whole country realized it was no longer business as usual. There was now a new sheriff in town.

The *kipande* laws were strictly enforced whereby everybody who traveled to the cities, towns and hamlets was required to show their pass book that identified not only who they were but also where they lived and who they worked for. People were required to explain their business if they were ever caught deviating from what their travel documents indicated. A law was also passed ordering all Kikuyu young men to leave Nairobi and those that did not heed the call soon enough were rounded up by the police. It is funny that even today the Kenya police code still has loitering laws in place that officers enforce by arresting their own people in the streets for not carrying this identity card document.

You see this *kipande* document also listed your tribe, because the natives were identified by their tribe, physical features, gender and unique body marks. So when these Kikuyu thugs started killing people, the government swept their lot out of the city and they were all detained in various parts of the country. One of my uncles, James Thuku, who otherwise worked as a cook for a white family in Nairobi and was then twenty-two years old, was caught up in the dragnet and detained in *Manyani,* a prison that had no barbed wire protection or these modern day gadgets because it was in the middle of a game park full of man eating lions. One was much safer inside the prison than anywhere else outside. The prison guards were more worried about wildlife than they were about the prisoners. In any event, the prison guards were also African and the prisoners were not necessarily criminals. My uncle used to claim how he had met several friends while at Manyani and these included people like the late J.M.Kariuki, a popular Kenyan politician whose death or assassination was associated by his supporters to the late president Jomo Kenyatta. Uncle, who worked as a cook while in detention and therefore commanded some measure of respectability, and I suspect this must have been his side of the story, used to pass writing materials to J.M. Kariuki, and through a complicated process of communication, the detainees were able to exchange correspondence with number Ten Downing Street in London, thereby notifying British politicians in England of how badly the settlers in Kenya were treating them.

It never stops to amuse me why these people would have had so much faith in the British legal system to the extent of not seeing the connection between their local administration and London. They appear to have been reconciled to the idea that the white Kenyans were part of that country. It does seem like they never wanted the British people to go away. Had the British turned around and created some acceptable systems that gave some measure of privileges if not full rights to the Africans, I think the Africans had no problem with colonialism. The rallying call for independence and freedom could not have been robust. My assessment, and I am only speculating, is that if there were any Africans that truly believed in the full liberation of their country, they must have been very few indeed. Why? Look at all the people who came to power upon independence! By the time of the emergency in '52 most of them were in school overseas with scholarships funded by the British government. I have in mind people like Charles Njonjo who became Kenya's first Attorney General. Mwai Kibaki, the current president, was at the London School of Economics. Jomo Kenyatta himself had just come back from London after 16 years. And what is even more telling is the fact that most of them were married to white women. I believe the spirit of liberation was perhaps only deeply felt in the minds of very few people and this perhaps not because of some well reasoned basis but perhaps due to some pent up desire for material accomplishment. Had the desire for freedom been so robust, all these tell tale signs would surely not have been present. What may be humiliating to Africans is the realization that what we see today must have been obvious to the British at that time. I believe this is the basis upon which so many of the British remained in that country after independence. The Africans must have, either due to ignorance, helplessness, fear, or short-term interest come to accept their situation in the colony. And this is also further evidenced by the post independence constitution, which was negotiated and hammered out at Lancaster house in London.

When the current president of Kenya got involved in a road accident during his campaign in 2002, he was rushed to hospital in London and this was not perceived as unusual in any way because this is what had happened since before independence. In fact, one of his presidential political rivals, upon losing his bid, also took a few months vacation in England to recuperate from campaign fatigue.

In The Thick of Things

In a nutshell therefore, when all is said and done, the *Mau Mau* group that gave their lives for the cause of their country's independence were nothing more than tribal thugs that only temporarily disturbed the peace that prevailed in that country before and after independence. A number of Africans would naturally have a problem with this and I know many people might want to condemn me for what I say. They are however entitled to their opinions, just as I am. I would dare whoever might want to throw the first stone to first show me the grave of Dedan Kimathi. Let them tell me why Kenyans do not have a graveyard dedicated to their freedom veterans.

But my intention is not to humiliate or expose the unpatriotic ways of some of my former countrymen or to provide some historical accounts of events because there are those that have spent years poring through books and researching, interviewing elders and so forth so as to have an accurate record of events. In any event, my own patriotism is whacky, having left and acquired the citizenship of some other country. And that country happens to be a British colony to this day.

The foregoing also must not be interpreted as a disguised attempt at appeasing the former colonialists for I have no reason to. I think their legacy created the breeding ground for all the pain that I have been through for so long. I particularly get upset when I meet Africans who pretend to run away from themselves. I was in church the other day, when a certain friend of mine who himself came from some third world country in the tropics proclaimed for all to hear that he had won some opportunity to travel to some country in Africa, although he would still cringe at the thought of finding spiders or some other crawling creatures. He would be going there, he announced, to help the Africans deal with the millions of AIDS orphans in that particular country. There are also those Africans who will pretend to or have already actually forgotten their mother tongues or have changed their names all in the naïve view that these maneuvers will help them get along in their careers or command more respect in their foreign communities. Some have not permitted their children to speak their mother tongue for they are ashamed that they may not be perceived as progressive. By the way, most women in Kenya who had converted to Christianity were reluctant to assist their husbands prepare and work on tobacco farms, even though their families did not have other reliable sources of generating cash at that time. My own mother only minded tobacco crops reluctantly because she could not convince dad why it was wrong for her to do it. Stuff like locally brewed African beer was deemed illegal and the earliest date I can remember seeing police officers is when my grandpa had prepared local brew following the marriage of one of my step aunts. He had invited his friends and family and had made this drink that they had always drunk since the world began. Then the police pounced and men were seen running full throttle grasping tenuously to their gourds of the drink of their ancestors, with the police officers in hot pursuit, in search of court evidence. Not many people wanted to fall outside the established system and I think this explains the awkward tendencies to impress foreigners.

I have also not forgotten that it was illegal in Kenya before independence for Africans to plant cash crops and this kept them poor and easy to manipulate and manage.

In The Thick of Things

I am also fearlessly aware that any lack of conviction on the part of the general population of their ability to change the colonial system was rooted in feelings of inadequacy and a lack of understanding planted in their souls by the colonial powers through the denial of sources of education and empowerment. This does not change the fact that most were reluctant to accept, let alone to fight and to struggle for their independence. I believe this is a historical fact that may not be changed by how we would want to look today. A good example is the case of my step grandfather on my mother's side who was a senior chief in colonial Kenya. This guy committed suicide when he heard that Kenyatta had been released from prison. I think he could not reconcile himself with black rule, either because he knew how much he had thrived on the basis of betraying the innocence of his people, or perhaps he feared the backlash that he could have faced for any wrongs that he may have committed to the people when protected by the power of high office. There is no shame that I am somehow related to a family that was so compromised and was a sell out. I think I have a basis for excusing these distant grandpas, uncles, and their wealthy families and the way they perceived their world in the context of their time. And in any event there were several others who were and are still just like them. In fact this is one of the reasons that I am writing this book. To debate and to try to seek an understanding of why people behave the way they do.

I went to Njiris high school for my secondary school education, as is still the practice in that country to send children to boarding schools away from home. I think this is an example of what some people might see as a benefit from the colonial system. The land on which my school stood was once owned by senior chief Njiri. When Njiri heard on the radio that independence was eminent he is infamously reputed to have struck his radio for communicating bad news to him. Like my step grandpa chief Jeremiah Ngari, and the name Ngari means leopard, chief Njiri's jurisdiction neighbored the Aberdare forest and the *Mau Mau* operated from that forest. I am sure the two chiefs must have lost thousands of goats and cattle and must have lived with terror and desperation for their own lives.

Kenya as I have demonstrated before is an exceedingly beautiful country and full of resources and once you have a good hold of some juicy portion you don't want to easily let go. I think this explains why the British went there and hanged on tenuously.

Chapter Five
Early Life and Bliss

Mabirikani—Mabirikani – number twenty—eight-- I went for a --walk but now I stop!—honor a break! I have no clue what the accurate English translation of mabirikani is or where in the large universe the game came from, but this did not matter to us or stop the song or the dance. We thus sang and danced as we skipped rope, or played *banya* outside our school dirt compounds during break time and on our way home and anywhere else where there was a gathering of two or more boys or girls. We would always say to each other, *"Let us go out to play banya"* if we ever found ourselves in an enclosed space especially with adults. Nobody ever said no to banya. By the way, banya is the corrupted Swahili name for a rat. So, since there was so much jumping and turning and skipping, perhaps the jumpers were meant to have been the banyas. Nobody wore any shoes and we would skid and fall and skid and fall and rise up and fall again. Not rain, high winds nor a teacher's cane would ever separate us from our game. Girls wore green or blue dresses with matching blouses and sweaters while boys wore khaki short pants, short sleeved shirts of the same color with blue sweaters. Looking back, I can only imagine that the dominant color of our clothes, I am sure now, must have been a dirty brown although it did not seem that way that time. I particularly thought I was always very clean and smart but since I can also remember that I was an extremely active child, I must reasonably assume that I was also not very different from anybody else.

Banya was especially liked by girls although boys also played it sometimes. The game involved taking turns to throw a plastic paper ball at one of us who would be in the middle, while at the same time one was also skipping some squares on one foot. The objective was to make sure that you dodged as many balls as possible while also not missing your step. This difficult juggling process ensured that all had a chance to play. There was great laughter and disappointments as the players were forced to change turns. Boys also used the same kind of soft plastic bags to make soccer balls and to practice dribbling skills.

Primary school compounds were the noisiest places especially during the early morning break and immediately after regular school when we went out for formal supervised sports. We competed this time with proper inflated cow hide soccer balls. I think the weight and hardness of these balls discouraged many kids from fully developing their soccer skills. I remember fearing to kick fully inflated balls because they were very heavy especially when it had rained because the leather would accumulate moisture. You did not want to be hit smack on the face particularly if you were prone to nose bleeding as was my case. You also did not want to get your toes caught up in the thread that tied down the air nozzle and tubing. I had also cut my big toe while kicking plastic paper ball soccer at home. Somebody had forgotten a machete on the grass outside our compound and my ball had landed on the sharp blade of the machete that was slightly covered by the grass. So this ball was at a nice angle and I went full force to kick the thing and whack! My toe was incised to the bone and blood gushed out in a smooth red jet. I can remember vaguely going to hospital and receiving a few stitches but I also remember applying a lot of that deep green plant's stuff that stopped bleeding in an instant. I also remember how the nail peeled away during the recovery process and how I developed this other softish nail that cracked whenever I did not trim it properly. More like the way a sheep's hooves crack if they are not trimmed for a long time. I think this was the reason that I never became a great soccer player although I could play goal keeper or a substitute defender. I enjoyed athletics, and some volleyball.

We did serious athletics in the second term of the school year which coincided with the cooler and wetter months of the year. We also played volleyball. Even our teachers at times competed against each other and this provided great excitement. I was an extremely good sprinter especially in the four hundred and eight hundred meter races. I competed all the way to the district level while in primary school and ran for my province in the inter-schools games during my high school years. I ran and beat police and military officers and took home many presents. I also loved hop, skip and jump from an early age because I had a very strong spring and could hop and skip farther than anybody else in my school especially as I became older.

To soften the landing for high jumpers, the school would have us bring sawdust that was used to fill up the jumping pit thereby improvising a biodegradable sponge. When there were no teachers, we would queue behind each other and make a continuous stream of small jumpers who would run back and jump again in a circuitous way. If you made a mistake and fell then the other jumpers would stampede on you and there was always plenty of fun and laughs. But accidents sometimes happened. This occurred to me, and for many years I had to nurse a bump on my collar bone that had been broken by all the small weights that landed on my neck as I lay in an awkward heap.

As there were always younger kids than ourselves and we were all in this very communal environment, we hardly ever cried and parents would only notice a problem when it was indeed very serious. I know I stayed with a broken collar bone at age eight for more than two days before my parents made a decision that the problem was well beyond home treatment. I was then carried by my father with my feet dangling over his face while I sat on his scapula for eight kilometers to the nearest hospital where the doctor decided that I needed more serious attention. I was then transferred to the provincial general hospital where they put a cast around my neck to hold the collar bone firmly. This gave me a nick name at school, *kaguku,* meaning the humped one, because the cast made it appear like I had a hump on my upper back.

But hump or no hump nobody ever wanted to miss school. It was the most exciting place to be. Teachers would at times beat us up when we made mistakes or when one was not paying enough attention or failed tests, but staying at home was never an option. Home was a lonely place to be and nobody actually ever stayed in the house during the day unless one was very sick or very advanced in age. There was always something more interesting to do out there away from the home compound. People only went to the house when it was either dark or it was raining heavily. A house was never an investment in rural Kenya and people spent nominal amounts of money to build houses. The environment was forever warm so there was never a need for heating and in any event there was no electricity or air conditioning to cool you down during the hotter months. If your home was in the mountains however, as ours was, temperatures lingered in the 20 degree Celsius range with a regular breeze so weather considerations were never a factor in peoples' lives. In fact nobody ever spoke about the weather. It was always a good day and it therefore never made sense for people to begin conversations with compliments or complaints about the weather. Houses were used as protection against water damage to the scant household property, and as protection against being rained on while people were asleep. Nobody ever slept during the day unless they were very sick. People did not work at night and this is the only time they used their houses. The whole damn place always shut down for twelve hours every single day of the year since the beginning of time for good or for worse.

It actually took me almost two years in Canada to really appreciate the notion that a house was such an important investment. It never quite sank in me when

Peter Mwangi

I heard so many people appearing so carried away about owning houses. And moreover, these were timber houses that cost almost nothing to build in Kenya. It did not excite me when it finally caught up with me that a house was actually going to be one of my greatest investments in North America if I was ever going to be lucky enough to find a good job.

To build a timber house in my childhood days, a man took a machete and an axe or a power-saw if he was more sophisticated. In the company of two or three friends he would then get into the woods, chop off one or two trees and split up the wood planks and bring them home. Within the next two to three days bingo, you had a new house. And unless one has had the opportunity to observe builders apply calking and building basements and considered the power of hurricanes and tornadoes or experienced an Alberta winter, the distinction between a cabin and a house is quite blurry. Most houses in modern Kenya are actually wooden cabins.

During my childhood days, most houses were mud huts with grass thatch. Men brought home the poles and rafters while women gathered thatching grass and prepared moist soil. Men would also gather twine from the bush and dug holes where they stuck in the shafts firmly into the ground. They would then firm up the structure by tying the rafters to the poles and made a cone shaped roof. Once their job was done, the womenfolk would put mud cake in the gaps between the rafts for the walls. They would also thatch the roof with special long thatching grass. A mixture of wood ash and cow dung thereafter would be used as calking to smooth the walls of the structure. This provided a seal against cracks once

In The Thick of Things

the mud dried up. The mixture also protected the wood from being infested by ants. The whole thing formed such a hard crust that white ants were never able to penetrate and such a house could last for upwards of twenty to thirty years. But its construction was a communal activity which took a day or two and only cost the owner a few kegs of home brewed beer and one or two goats that would be feasted upon by the community once the house was ready for occupation.

There was an alternative to the use of cow dung and ash. One could buy a few bags of cement and mix mud with the moist soil to make and seal the walls. Then instead of having a dirt floor, people at times gathered river-bed rocks, knock them down into ballast that would be beaten down into the ground. Once a relatively smooth surface formed, then cement mixed with ochre or red paint would be applied to the smoothened surface. Some people did the smoothening business quite well while others were not so good. At times people actually tripped their toes over on some jutting uneven surface inside their houses. Such accidents were however rare. Furthermore, this floor smoothening business was never too popular as the cement made the house too cold at night and helped retain puddles of water as some people also sometimes used their bedrooms as their shower rooms. With a mud floor there was no flooding because the dry ground would soak in the water in a few hours and perhaps because of the slow drying process the floor became quite hard and it was never dusty so long as the house was occupied all the time. But if a house had not been occupied for some time, dust gathered on everything and one needed to splash a lot of water before any attempt at sweeping the floors as you could easily suffocate. The windows were narrow and criss-crossed with the rafters which circled the circumference of the hut. You did not want to cut these because your action might weaken the whole structure.

I think there was also another practical reason that the windows were kept narrow. Sheep and goats were also kept inside the house. And I am now starting to think about the greenhouse effect as I reflect on this arrangement. Just imagine how it was like to have fifty goats and twenty sheep all crowded inside this hut. Imagine also a nursing mother with a young infant at the other corner of the hut. But I think they may have dealt with the gassing problem by sizing the hut based on the number of inhabitants that were going to be dwelling therein. Whenever I visited my grandfather's place, I always saw the sheep at a respective distance in the *"kweru"* meaning the white corner because in the dark surroundings of the hut you were always able to pick out a goat or a sheep in a certain corner because of their white teeth. But there were wild animals such as leopards and hyenas roaming outside particularly at night. Although these were never such a big threat to human beings for I do not know anybody who was ever killed by a wild animal despite the many encounters, they were a real threat to livestock. In the event the window was too large and somebody left it open by mistake, you could always entertain an unwelcome guest. And you can be sure, once a leopard was in a sheep's pen; it was never going to get out hungry. So people had to be cautious. The wild animals could also try to dig below the foundation although this was rare. Those villagers who resulted to improvising rocky surfaces on their floors of their houses were actually driven to these actions by a desire to protect their animals from the intruders particularly during the late seventies when competition for land between man and wildlife intensified following increased planting of cash crops and clearing of many bushes that had previously provided food and camouflage for antelopes and deer among other prey for the meat eaters.

All said, building a house in rural Kenya was just a regular community activity and never called for municipal, local government and zoning arrangements and no houses ever collapsed on anybody.

Even though I had owned a house in Nairobi, it was really never such a big deal and we had paid our mortgage in about eight years. What mattered more to my community was to own land, because one could plant crops or rear domestic animals on it. Land to most Kenyans was a source of income, not just a place where you built a house. And these ideas were formed at a very early age based on what everybody in the village thought and practiced. There is a tautology in Kenya that says that once a villager one was always a villager and that you could take a villager to the city but you would never be able to remove the village out of the villager!

If you ever got sick at night, you either waited for day break or if your case became too serious and you did not find enough help to carry you to hospital, then you died. And it was just that simple. There were however, few people who succumbed due to lack of an ability to reach medical attention in the wee hours of the night in the fifteen years that I lived permanently in the village during my early childhood and primary school days. In fact few people were ever seriously sick. My grandfather was one of those guys who kicked the bucket but his case was a special one. Like most old people, grandpa did not want to be taken to the hospital. He wanted to die at home. In any event, it would have been a waste of time and effort taking him to hospital because he would never have voluntarily agreed to swallow medicine. He would have wanted to know what medicine it was for he believed he knew the taste of all the plants and roots that were used as medicine. There was, for instance the *mugaita* tree roots that were boiled to cure all stomach ailments. There were *mahuitia* that cured swellings and tumors and blue gum tree leaves that were boiled to cure fevers. There were also several other herbs and roots that people like grandpa mixed with bone soup to cure other ailments and to strengthen the body's immune system against viral and bacterial infections. In fact doctors always warned people against taking "home" medicine while also taking hospital medicine because these could counter each other's effects or make you sicker and untreatable. I think my grandpa would have been untreatable for he had not taken any modern medicines for ninety six years if the guesswork that went into determining his age was anywhere accurate. They said that he was of the *kihiu mwiri* age group and since people like Jomo Kenyatta who could tell roughly when they were born also belonged to that age group, and my grandpa could also vividly recall the events of the First World War, it was therefore easy to make an intelligent estimate regarding when he was born.

The third term in the school year was dedicated to serious academic pursuit and preparation for final school year exams. It had to be this way particularly because we had only one chance to pass the final primary school exams, the passing or failure of which was the determining factor as to whether one proceeded to high school as well as the quality of the high school. Competition for high school spots was therefore stiff. The best high schools were government run boarding schools and these were few and far from home. We spent every three months away from home, with a one week mid-term break, for three terms in a year. Boys would go to boys' only boarding schools and girls to girls' only boarding schools. This made both girls and boys very shy with each other during the school holidays. There wasn't too much dating. But there was a lot of letter writing to each other during the school year. We would write to each other about how plentiful our love for each other was with descriptive words like the sand in the sea or like all the stars in the skies or like all the leaves in the forest but we would have nothing to say to each other when we finally met. Just looking at each other was enough to cause flight. If you were a little more composed and gathered enough courage to talk to a girl, you had to be very careful what you said lest you crossed the line and scared the hell out of her. She would leave you alone and never talk to you again. If you were more polished and you actually managed not to scare away your potential girlfriend, because no girl would ever admit to a boy that she was actually that boy's girlfriend, lest he became too big headed and spread the 'gossip' to his boy folk, she would be digging a hole in the ground with her big toe as she spoke inaudibly and softly to you with her eyes firmly rooted on the ground. But don't get fooled. She was always doing some girly mathematics as she did her toe digging activity.

For starters, no girl would ever have agreed to meet you during the day and you only noticed that she was digging holes on the ground if there was moonlight. In addition, the meetings would normally take place within a reachable distance from her home. Furthermore, before any serious dating could begin, she would always demand that you visited her at her home in the presence of her parents. Assuming you were courageous enough and most boys were and you actually visited, and her parents did not appear to have a problem with you being the boyfriend of their daughter, then the harder part would follow. The girl's parents gave you several hints that they had no problem with you, and this was not necessarily a good thing, for it could also have meant that they were not too sure about the character of their daughter, such that it was better the devil they knew than the saint they had not yet met. The father would normally share some of his childhood stories and monitor your reaction as to whether you were getting interested or you were showing boredom. He could also show interest in your academic performance and would enquire about your school progress and your activities during the holidays. He may even share some home brewed beer with you, very friendly gestures indeed. The girls could get too flattered that they were now seeing a side of their father that they never thought he had. They also did not like him treating you like you were already a son in law for this might get you bloated and you instead lost your caution and manners towards them during their moment of containing your boyish attitudes. Mothers on the other hand would at such times busy themselves with kitchen chores and let their daughter spend time with you and her husband. They spoilt you and created every opportunity for studying and understanding you in the shortest time possible. In the event your visit had not been previously announced, and most of them were not, the mother would even ask her daughter to see you off to the gate in the event the daughter was showing shyness and reluctance lest it be perceived that it was she who had actually invited you to their home in the first place. If you were indeed an unwanted intruder, the girl would make sure that this point was firmly driven home by either going to sleep when you are having a field day with her parents, or she would simply go out visiting with other neighborhood girls while you at her home. You would thereafter never garner the courage to ever again go to her home in the pretext that you were actually visiting her.

The harder part for the boy and the one that girls really thoroughly enjoyed was visiting your parents. She could unceremoniously just show up in your home and join your mother in whatever tasks your mother was doing. Most boys would run away from home at such times. This was really a particularly difficult time if you were not quite serious with the girl in the first place. And women have a special way of relating with each other. The same girl, who may have appeared coy, would of a sudden be laughing and joking and screaming about as she exchanged jokes with your mother and your sisters while you hurdled as far away from this group as you could. You were however always interested with the indirect feedback you got from your feminine relatives. Some might tell you directly that so and so was a nice girl or your mother may in fact subsequently invite the same girl again to come do some chores in your home without your knowledge. You will only one day see the girl working in the fields in the company of your parents. In fact you may not even be at home when these things happened.

If you thought matters were going too far, and most boys in high school never wanted these relationships to progress that far, you may result to directly confronting your girlfriend and demanding that she desist visiting with your female relatives especially with your mother. You also disapproved anything positive your sisters said about the 'scheming' girlfriend. This would henceforth become part of your points of weakness that your sisters would use to tease you.

Matters however at times went the other way and somebody's daughter became pregnant. You had few choices as a young man. The lady would have built enough evidence to prove that you were indeed the father of the unborn child. Every single woman in the village including your mother and the girl's mother would by this time have accumulated overwhelming information concerning your relationship. In the event you were not ready for marriage, then you would have to make arrangements for the child to be taken care of by your mother at your expense or at your family's expense. The young mother could however decide to keep the baby and continue living with her parents until a reasonable time when you would find a means to support her and the child. If the girl did not decide that it was all a mistake and move on, then you would have to take mother and child and begin a family as soon as you had the capacity to support them. You could also be taken through the customary dispute handling process and be fined as appropriate. The child was, however, always a father's responsibility and even if the mother decided to keep the child, upon maturity the child could choose to rejoin its father. If the father died in the meantime, the clan would allocate some resources to the child for there is a saying that "*rika na nyumba itiumagwo*" meaning that nobody is ever able to escape or to vacate his age group or his clan.

Primary school days were however much better and never complicated by these teenage issues.

All over rural Kenya, people did not have to own any watches because they were always able to tell the time by following the rhythm in the schools. If my mother was plucking tea, she would know when it was ten in the morning because she could hear the bell ring followed by a big roar and outpouring as the kids ran out of their classrooms.

Unlike in North America, because of warm conditions of Africa, schools in Kenya are on open compounds and most people live in the rural areas where there is minimal noise pollution and sound is heard very far away. There is also a primary school every three to five kilometers and pupils walk to and from school. For some reason, schools were always built on higher grounds, I think because it was easier to make it flat for the play fields. Most homes were on parallel level ground with the schools across a river or a stream and people would normally work on the farms overlooking the school. If I ever looked carefully I was always able to see my parents on the farm at home and they in turn could here me if I shouted or hollered in school.

Everybody also knew everybody and even grade one students didn't need their parents' escort to or from school because there were always neighborhood kids to provide company. In fact kids never went home without finding each other because they were friends and playmates. Friendships would have been formed many years before becoming of school age at six, seven or eight depending on body size and your willingness to go to school. The teachers tested whether we were ready for school by asking us to touch our ear lobe with the opposite hand stretched over the head. If your hand was too short and you did not touch your ear lobe then you stayed at home until your hand was long enough.

Handicraft was another skill that all kids learnt in primary school. Girls did crochetwork and needlework. They were also taught home economics, cooking and basic hygiene. Boys on the other hand learnt how to make sculptures of wood or stone and made artifacts. We carved wood and stone wildlife and caricatures of people. We also made tea baskets using tree branches and natural twine. I was especially good in this and had a small side business at an early age. I used to make many tea baskets and would display my wares on tea paydays in the buying centers where farmers went to cash in their monthly pay. With these proceeds I was always able to buy clothes and to pay for my school fees from an early age. You made the bags in the fields while looking after your parent's livestock or during the evenings just before dusk. If you were a side business boy as I was, you could also do your *rugara* weaving in the moonlight outside. You could also make a hurricane lantern and buy kerosene. As soon as home work was done, I would keep myself busy for a few more hours working my baskets until eleven every night.

In The Thick of Things

We also had a lot of other fun times at home. Once the cows were milked and penned in, it was time for story telling, metaphor and riddle interpretations. We would tell both true and imaginary stories. The scarier the stories the better they were because there was no electricity, and the nights, unless there was moonlight, used to be very dark especially if it was also raining. Parents and especially grandmas would pretend that they did not know that they were making us get scared and they would choose the darkest nights to tell us the most frightening tales of the wolf and the goat with her seven kids. "Once upon a time there lived mother goat and her seven kids", the story would begin. "Mother goat planned on a journey to the market to have her maize ground for *ugali* and porridge flour. She would warn the kids against opening the door for anybody other than herself. As she gave these instructions and warnings, the wolf would be hiding by the corner of the house and it would hear everything from the small gaps in the walls of the house. And this was the reason why it was always said that walls had ears and people never gossiped about others at night.

As soon as mother goat had left the home compound, the wolf would come and knock at the door. *Knock. Knock. Knock.* "Who is it?" the kids would ask in unison. "It is me, your mother", the wolf would respond in that wolf voice. Then the kids would say, "We are not going to open, we know your voice wolf, go away!" Then the wolf would go away and practice as much as possible to sound like mother goat.

The wolf would try again, except this time the kids would get fooled by the voice which would be just like their mother's. "Mee, Mee, it is me your mother. Are you alright my dear kids? I have come with bananas, yams and cassava. Please open the door for your mother". The temptation to open would be great and there would be silent arguments as to whether to immediately open or not. Then finally common sense would prevail and they would ask the mother to show one of her hooves to prove that it was indeed she. Then driven by excitement about the opportunity to have the door opened, the wolf would forget about its claws and would show one of its paws, complete with those frightening knives. The kids would together scream in fright at having been almost duped and would chase away the wolf thus, "You are not our mother, you are the wolf, we have seen your claws." The wolf would not give up but would this time would become very inventive. In addition to keeping mother goat's voice, it would also go home and dip its paws in white corn flour and then come back again.

It would make the same plea as before but would also show its flour covered front foot with the claws tightly pulled back into the paws and become adamant that it was indeed the mother and threaten to go away and leave the kids alone hungry if they did not open. In confusion, the kids would open and one by one they would get eaten by the wolf. Mother goat would come home to find the house door open and the kids missing.

We would sleep very scared and a few of us screamed in the night in fear of being eaten by the wolf.

Then we would also tell riddles and these would begin as follows: "*Gwata ndai. Gwata ugwatiriire. Nguheo ki? Ndakuhe Kirima kia Nyandarwa na nyamu ciakio ciothe. Ndathii uu, ndathii uu? Njira cia ategi.* The riddle teller would begin by announcing that she was about to tell a riddle. And for emphasis the speaker would repeat again that she was about to tell a riddle. She would also want to know what her pay was going to be for telling the riddle. If you were interested to listen then you gave a very substantial reward, in this case the entire Aberdare Ranges, previously known as the Nyandarwa Mountains and all the wildlife in it. Since the gift is considered sufficient then the asker poses the riddle which in this case is "I go this way and then that way?" The answer is *"njira cia ategi"* meaning the paths of the hunters that criss-cross each other. *My house has no door? An egg. I have a friend who never leaves me? A shadow. My house has one pole? A mushroom plant. I will marry when women stop gossip? A catholic priest. I will get circumcised at a time of my choosing? A Luo warrior. My girlfriends are forever beautiful? A he goat. My grandmother mourns for me every night? The owl. My friend has a stealthy step? A snake. My journey never ends? A circle.*

The evenings were also a good time for competing in chanting, memorizing and interpreting metaphors such as *There is no thief or the one who looks out for him. He, who never heeds advice, chooses not how to receive castigation. He who keeps company of the wayward also becomes wayward. An obedient baby never misses somebody to clean him up. He, who is on a self destructing path, never finds a friend good enough to guide him back to sobriety. A baby that refuses the care of its mother never makes it. Nobody enjoys trouble other than a thief and a witch. A good club develops from its base. A dancer is never praised at home. A good warrior is not necessarily the one with the largest biceps. A powerful warrior gets brought down by a maize cob.*

We also sung songs about our ancient heroes and prophets. We would at such times also sing freedom songs such as the following "*Chege wa Kibiru nioigiri thingira uria uri Kiawairera, riria ugakwo na urike norio tukona wiyathi. Bururi uyu witu Gikuyu Ngai ni aturathimiire na akiuga tutikoima kuo.* In other words, *"Our ancient sage, Chege son of Kibiru, prophesied that when the elder's mansion at Kiawairera is finally constructed and ready for occupation this will be the only time that we shall finally get our independence. This is our blessed land of the Gikuyu people that God gave us and commanded us to never ever surrender to anybody else.* The *thingira* in Kiawairera was supposed to be the mini-state house in Jomo Kenyatta's home village in Gatundu division of Kiambu district of Kenya. A child's sense of pride and identification with the country's history was powerfully communicated in song, rhythm and dance as we sat by the hearth awaiting dinner because nobody ever had dinner during daylight hours. People worked on their farms until dark and when it was no longer possible to be out, we hurdled by the log fire always in the middle of the hut.

In these and several other ways the society educated its people about the values of obedience, respect for authority, patriotism and their culture in the absence of modern day interruptions involving Hollywood celebrities and soap operas.

Also, when we were not very busy in the fields, especially during the weekends, we used to go out trapping wildlife such as guinea fowl and geese. Guinea fowls particularly liked eating worms on the wet ground in the bush where large trees like the *mugumo* tree of the fig family would provide substantial overgrowth that would completely prevent sunlight from reaching all the areas beneath the canopy of these giant trees. When the birds were under this canopy, they would be on the ground in the bush and still have adequate view of their surroundings. We would get in there and lay our traps. I am not sure that I ever caught anything but I know some people who did. The guinea fowls are no fools and for you to succeed in trapping and catching them, you had to be very good in camouflaging any tell-tale signs that yours was a trap. And many guys in grades three or four were never this good.

I remember one day, and I think I was about ten or so, when we went on this guinea fowl trapping mission with my older brother who was two years my senior. We had just begun putting the sticks together at the base of this giant *mugumo* tree when I looked up. First I saw the eyes. Then my brother noticed that I was looking up and so he also looked. Then I saw the spots, and when he said that he could also see a wagging tail, we bolted. We both knew we were in imminent danger. A leopard had at all this time been looking down at us even as we gathered our stupid small sticks for trapping the elusive guinea fowls. We fled like the wild fire. The ground was wet and sloping all the way to the river below that was all covered with clippers and twigs and overhanging bushes. We could only go one way- upwards, and we slipped, fell, stood, ran, slipped and rose again until we were out of the woods.

As all this drama happened I am sure the leopard must have been just laughing and having it easy for it did not bulge. As soon as we were at a safe distance, we began screaming that we had seen a leopard. When my father, who was the quickest to respond, came over, he took aim and flung a machete into the tree where we described the animal to have been hiding. We saw the cat leap down and disappear into the woods.

Nobody ever mentioned, let alone holler, a leopard's name in vain. There was this old story about a boy who always used to holler, *uii Ngari i! Uii Ngari i! mutiuke Mundeithie uii Ngari i! Ui Ngari!* Meaning come and help me, come and help me, I am about to be killed by a leopard. People would go quickly to help him only to find that there was no leopard, and that the boy would only have been joking. So when he finally did encounter a leopard and he was attacked, nobody took him seriously or responded to his screams in good time. When they finally did, it was too late, and the boy had already been mauled down. There was also a saying that 'a leopard is only hunted by a man in the company of his in-laws', meaning that since the animal is too swift and fierce, you have to be such trusting friends so that you cannot abandon each other while in trouble. A marriage relationship was expected to cultivate such a strong bond of friendship. No man was expected to be so mean as to think of abandoning his father in-law in danger, and vice versa.

We also did business in our own small ways. When my mother's younger brother completed high school and began working for the paramilitary police in Nairobi, he lived in the barracks and rarely came home. He wanted to get married and that meant he had to plant tea bushes that his wife would take care of, for wives never followed their husbands to the cities those days. People, mainly men, worked in the cities and came home to the rural areas every Friday where their families lived.

In The Thick of Things

Employment income was supplemental to *home* income. It was also the man's responsibility to build a house and find a stable activity for his wife before he got married. Under these circumstances, my uncle needed his land tilled and planted with tea bushes a few years before he was ready to marry. I must have been probably twelve or thirteen. I requested that I be permitted to dig up all the grass and prepare this virgin eight acre piece of land for the planting of tea bushes. When I got the opportunity, I divided up the land into small chunks and subcontracted these to my school mates. Within a week the whole place was cultivated and ready for planting. I did not do any digging myself which was a taxing exercise that left your hands blistered, but I was able to make a very good profit that was used to buy all the books that I needed and to defray a significant portion of my form one school fees. Form one was the first year of high school and the equivalent to grade nine in North America.

Once in high school life took a more serious tone.

Majority of the students went to boarding schools several hours away from home and mingled with young people from across the country. Tribal hegemonies were played down and we interacted on the basis of vested interests in academic, sports and other extra curricula pursuits. There were no grandparents to give us monkey stories in the evenings. We had to follow the school routine for three blocks of three months each every year and only returned to our homes in the months of December, April and August while on school holidays.

We participated in various community activities including organizing church choirs, plays and drama during the school holidays. We helped our parents on the farms and did all kinds of manual jobs to find school fees which were needed on the first day back to school.

School holidays were also the time that teenagers met their potential future spouses. Boys and girls actively sought each other for everybody wanted to have a story once we were back in school. It was never cool for any teenager not to have a significant other; a *spice*, because having a spouse at this time would have been frowned upon.

There was only one university in the whole country and competition for space at campus was stiff. Students were required to not only pass very well in the general high school exams but also to spend another two years in advanced high school where we were also required to pass with top grades before proceeding to university. In the midst of abject poverty few parents had the financial resources to help their kids pass through all the hoops and barriers that a youngster was required to overcome before being able to acquire a university education. To many young people, the choices were few. You either dropped out of the school system or found yourself a job that paid you peanuts for the rest of your life, or bankrupted your parents through advanced high school and college where after you would find a middle level job. The option of finding work and or finding student loans to pursue school was not available, and many dreams were shattered in this way.

Like many young people across Africa, I fell in the group that passed their exams so well but could nevertheless not pursue my dream of one day becoming a medical doctor because of a lack of school fees. Unlike the majority of these poor souls however, I was able to find a reasonably good job and to dedicate myself to life-long learning.

In The Thick of Things

Through a complicated process of professional and academic pursuits, I finally got admitted to the University of Wales for PhD studies on Banking Efficiency effective September 2002 but unfortunately could not find the needed funding for these studies.

At the age of forty four, I think I am one of the oldest students at a local community college, pursuing some designation in accounting and finance although I already have post graduate qualifications in the same areas in the hope that by being involved in the community, I will enhance my visibility, remain current and not miss out on evolving local opportunities. My other motivating consideration and concern is that perhaps employers discount distance learning studies, or recruiters are not able to relate my work experience and academic qualifications or simply because they hate my African connection and are therefore reluctant to invite me for appropriate job interviews in Canada. The few that have interviewed me acknowledge that I have an extremely good resume, a confident and outgoing personality but for some reason only best known to them have not felt able to give me any jobs for more than one year now. And I have knocked on very many doors.

In a determined effort of refusing to give up and in yet one more attempt at remaining relevant and possibly to be able to one day establish another business of my own, I have calculated that I may have to obtain a more locally understood professional designation and have sought and received several exemptions for the Certified General Accountants examinations and hence my enrolment with the community college that enables me to receive government funding which would not be forthcoming if I read from home as I have done for other professional designations including the Chartered Financial Analysts designation that I am halfway through. To the extent that my government has agreed to fund sub-optimal courses in the same profession that they assessed my skills for before permitting me to immigrate to Canada implies that the left hand may not always know what the right hand is doing. Society resources are being misdirected. Just as I thought the Africans were sub optimizing their resources I have reason to believe it is not any different here in Canada. My society has the ability to follow through and disentangle obvious bottlenecks in our systems that are holding back the full potential of our economy. I dare speculate that the dismal performance on this score is based on some old fashioned attitudes about "us and them". I believe the "we" may be those who may consider themselves the thoroughbreds of society with a psychological expectation of being entitled for service from others who they may consider human species of the lower kinds; a continuation of the class system in vogue in Europe centuries ago. I believe this could be the kind of confusion that makes us unable to fully appreciate the pain of others as we have become used to the notion that some people were born to serve others. A small paradigm shift would have profound positive results. But I realize that any beneficiary of the status quo is realistically not able to feel the pain of others and the system may never change if the sufferers never speak up. To this extent, I consider it my responsibility to invite my society to look about itself so that we can take the urgently needed remedial steps to eliminate injustices in our midst.

Chapter Six

Canada, the True North Strong and Free

"Hi! Hello! Hello! You freaking sucker!" the girl said when she noticed that I had ignored her. I assumed I was not hearing and continued with the brisk step that I always used when walking alone at night. This was at 97 Street in downtown Edmonton where I first lived for the first three months after arriving in Canada. 97th Street was actually not my first residence because I had also spent a month at Econo lodge also in the down town. My security guard duties ended at about midnight and since there were few buses at that hour and because neither did I drive nor could afford a taxi, I used to walk home.

It had never crossed my mind that I was ever a freak, a coward, a sucker. No, she did not mean me. She must have been referring to my shadow. In any event it was already past midnight and she was at a respectable distance for her to notice it was really me. I also knew she was just looking for an escort and since I did not seem interested with whatever stuff she was strutting I had be a freak. Or maybe that is what I was; a freak, but more on this later.

I had harboured the idea that I could one day emigrate from Africa for many years, but this was always really just a notion. This was just a mental alternative that, if events for some reason did not work out well, I could fall back on. A focus on this option, however, developed a new urgency in 2001 when my hotel business in downtown Nairobi was demolished. I quickly sold my house, searched and found the Canadian embassy and put through an application to immigrate. I relocated from Nairobi to rural Kenya where I promoted investments in the money and capital markets. Looking back, this was the happiest time of my life and most rewarding part of my career. I was my own boss and the business was shaping up nicely. But it was also a very challenging moment financially, and staying the course when other opportunities were beckoning became unbearable, so I quit.

After working in the financial services industry in Kenya for over sixteen years, and travelling all over that country in various commercial lending positions, I had come to admire the determination, freedom and financial rewards that businesspeople appeared to enjoy. I had then reasoned that with my experience, knowledge and training it was quite possible and easy for me to set up on my own. Furthermore, I had seen how the wave of business restructuring and reorganization had shunned out unprepared bank employees into the streets at most unfortunate times in their careers. But the Swahili have sayings that *ukiona vikielea ujue vimeundwa* and *mtaka cha mvunguni sharti ainame. T*hey also say that *bahati ya* *mwenzio usiilalie nje*. These sayings mean that when you see beautiful vessels sailing in the seas always recognize that somebody has spent time and genius to make them that beautiful and furthermore the fortunes of one man are not necessarily going to be the fortunes of another. They also mean that for you to reach that which is beneath the bed, you must stoop down to pick it.

My wife Mary and I learnt these lessons the hard way because our café business located in an extremely busy part of Nairobi was demolished by the land owner, a crown corporation, after we had operated the business for only three months. Our landlord had leased the land from the Coffee Board of Kenya and in turn had subleased the properties to various people including ourselves.

We had mortgaged our home and borrowed one million Kenya shillings ($20,000) that we used to set up our extremely profitable café business. Unfortunately, the landlord was not remitting to the crown corporation and we went in, innocently, at a time when the tug of war between the two parties was at a climax. The crown corporation flexed its muscles and we suffered considerable damage. As the Swahili also say, *Ndume wawili wakipigana aumiaye ni nyasi*. This means that when two bulls fight the grass suffers. We had a five year lease document but we had long known that the reason Kenya, like other third world countries, has retrogressed is because of the failure of the state to recognize and enforce the supremacy of human and property rights. We had the option of sticking around to pursue our case through the court system and pay substantial amounts of money to lawyers and wait for years before the corrupt system finally decided our case. We could also quickly explore all sensible options available to us and move on. We chose the latter. And life to most people in less developed countries is about choosing the lesser of many evils. I believe this is how poverty for the majority is manufactured- through the transfer of wealth belonging to the masses to a small privileged minority. Yes, we transferred $20,000 of our life long savings, our genius and three months of hard labour to the Munyingi family and their cronies because we could not afford to pursue our rights in court.

Because the Canadian embassy in Nairobi was always inundated with visa applications, in a poor country the surest way they ensured that they only processed serious applications was to impose requirements that qualified applicants not only paid the needed landing and application processing fee upfront but also demonstrated that they had adequate funds to sustain them in Canada for the first six months, the kind of rather misleading hint they gave you concerning the longest time frame you would have to wait before finding work in your chosen profession. I dare say this was a deliberate lie. Even government jobs discount certain overseas experience especially that gained in Africa. For those of us in finance, most jobs will ask for, among other things, in addition to undergraduate or graduate qualifications, local professional qualifications such as the CGA, Certified General Accountant, a Canadian qualification, or the CFA, Certified Financial Analyst, that until recently has been a purely North American qualification. Majority of immigrants will not have heard about these qualifications let alone having obtained them. One gets the impression of having been hoodwinked to come over to do manual jobs as cooks, personal support workers, security guards and other similar occupations. This is compounded by the fact that the distinction between refugees and landed immigrants from Africa is negligible. In fact, I think refugees may even be better off because they come under the direct care of the government, so they do not have to go through all the hoops that landed immigrants go through.

What infuriates me more even as I write this section is the realization that even as these things happen, the embassy will have taken in your resume, oh, sorry, I mean your curriculum vitae as they call it out there, and in some cases will even have interviewed you, so there would be no question about the suitability of one's qualifications. The government of Canada is clearly able to know the chances of one finding a job in Canada by the time they issue your immigrant visa. The applicant is never told in explicit terms exactly when their application process is to be completed. They give you a timeframe in months pertaining to the earliest time that you must wait before calling in to enquire on the application. I was given thirteen months. Yes, this is the time I waited before the approval of my visa application to transfer another $20,000 to Canada and to begin a new life; as a gas station attendant, a security guard and later a bank teller. This gets at you because there are many people in this country with the title 'manager' who have never attended school beyond grade twelve! How can we allow these injustices to exist in our society? Have we not learnt anything from our past?

Because of these embassy requirements, I determined that it was only financially feasible if I restricted my application to myself in the hope that once I was happily settled in Canada, I would then sponsor my family over. I now know I was looking out at a mirage, a pipe dream that I was hoodwinked to confuse with reality, just in the same way that so many others have been duped.

To ensure that the bank account retained enough funds for the Canadian embassy purposes, we laid low and avoided all activities that would have risked its depletion. Rather than pursuing our legal rights against our landlord in Nairobi, or setting up another business, we left Nairobi for rural Kenya where the cost of living is negligible. I spent the time doing semi-charitable work. I formed a consulting company and spent the next one year in Othaya, the nearest town to my rural place of birth. I organized conferences and met with teachers from all the ten high schools and over twenty primary schools in my neighbourhood. Mary provided office and moral support as I made these travels. I also published a quarterly journal that I distributed mostly for free to the community in various cities including Nairobi. I educated the community on the benefits of investing in the stock exchange and how they could make commercial banks more responsive to them by moving deposits to other investment opportunities. I used any spare time to teach accounting and banking to students who were preparing for exams since my office had significant free space. I felt an obligation to my community to help them lift their lot from poverty by making right investment choices. Since I was going to use my knowledge of finance overseas, I felt an urge to bequeath a portion of that to my own community. I felt patriotic, philanthropic, and even philosophical, a very satisfying sense of intellectual fulfilment. But you can only do certain things for so long.

In The Thick of Things

When the thirteen months were over, and there was no news from the Canadian embassy, I gave up the wait.

We had an undeveloped piece of land that we had purchased several years before. My mind was made up. I knew I could develop this land and get fully committed to organizing and educating the community for I had by this time earned some reasonable commissions from the people that I had persuaded to invest in the stock exchange. I went ahead and embarked on the project to build a reasonably beautiful house on my land in Kerugoya, on the foothills of Mount Kenya. This was the fruit of my labour. I had worked for every penny that went into this land. I was yet again extremely fulfilled.

Just when my contractor was fixing the roof, my cell phone rang. It was Mary with the news that a letter had arrived from the Canadian embassy advising that my immigration visa was successful and that I was required to go pick it up. I completed the house, had the water well dug up, completed fencing off, tilling and the planting of the first crop. I then moved my family over to our new home. I flew out of Jomo Kenyatta international airport in Nairobi on January 30th 2003. I arrived in Edmonton the following day as time zones quicken the journey when you fly out west.

"Welcome to Canada", the brightly smiling lady said as she completed stamping all my landed immigrant documents. She gave me a bundle of booklets and pamphlets that covered myriad topics including where to find an immigrant serving community and the process of becoming a Canadian citizen and websites for where I could go to find a job.

Peter Mwangi

As soon as I buckled the seat belt, I read as many of the booklets as quickly as I could. I was impressed with almost everything that I was reading. I was particularly impressed with the words of the national anthem and I went over them several times. My decision to come to Canada was vindicated. It was an especially powerful and friendly well thought out piece. I saw these words as reflective of the will and the dominant mindset of the people. I was immediately persuaded by this beautiful piece of the Canadian national anthem that appeared to communicate powerfully the national psyche. I would repeat again and again the words:

> O Canada!
>
> Our home and native land!
> True patriot love in all thy sons command.
> With glowing hearts we see thee rise,
> The True North strong and free!
> From far and wide,
> O Canada, we stand on guard for thee.
> God keep our land glorious and free!
> O Canada, we stand on guard for thee.
> O Canada, we stand on guard for thee.

As an immigrant, Canada's national anthem welcomes you. I had a small notebook that had the words of the Kenya national anthem and I placed that portion side by side and compared Kenya's national anthem with Canada's. I found the differences in attitude and national character to be significant. I would quietly hum and listen to the words of Kenya's national anthem and conduct a mind comparison with Canada's.

In The Thick of Things

> O God of all creation
> Bless this our land and nation
> Justice be our shield and defender
> May we dwell in unity
> Peace and liberty
> Plenty be found within our borders
>
> Let one and all arise
> with hearts both strong and true
> Service be our earnest endeavour
> And our homeland of Kenya
> Heritage of splendour
> Firm may we stand to defend
>
> Let all with one accord
> In common bond united
> Build this our nation together
> And the glory of Kenya
> The fruit of our labour
> Fill every heart with thanksgiving

Canada's national anthem asserts our right to our home and native land while Kenya's on the other hand appears to be taking their homeland for granted and starts with a prayer for God's blessings.

Canadians also, in their national anthem, acknowledge that we are immigrants and hence the verse on coming from far and wide. In addition, Canada's anthem also praises the strength and the freedom of our nation. It creates in one a sense of pride and place in the world community. It energizes you and provides you with a consoling calmness and reassurance as a new Canadian. The national anthem includes each one of us. At least on this one I have no doubt. I am not sure that the First

Nations people would share my sentiment but this again is another story.

I asked the taxi driver to take me to the nearest hotel by the airport since it was already dark. I also asked him to fetch me the following morning for he was going to be my guide, a role that he happily accepted. I enjoyed an extremely sound sleep that night. But I was also finding the place rather expensive. I think from the airport to the nearest Holiday Inn or whatever accommodation facility it was, I paid fifty dollars, almost ten times what I should otherwise have had to pay. What I ordered for dinner and breakfast is a completely different story for I did not have the vaguest clue concerning the cuisine in my new homeland. But I was ready to learn and to bring out the best in me for I had heard that North America was a land of opportunity for those who were prepared to work hard. I had never doubted my capacity to go the extra mile. Whatever it was going to take, my motto was always that so long as other people could do it, I was confident I could also do it. My bewilderment, however, began on the second day in the morning of January 31st 2003.

The whole place was covered in ice and my driver sloshed through to downtown Edmonton as I enjoyed the heat of his taxi.

The variety of subtle differences was staggering to say the least. While everybody spoke English, it was one of a different kind. Where I would have said *reverse*, they said *back up*. Back up to me meant an alternative plan, a reserve to fall back on should the first plan not work out. Like my back up plan concerning immigration. Where I would have said *curriculum vitae*, they said *resume* and where I would have said the *boot* of a car, they said *trunk* and the *bonnet* became the *hood*. A *lorry* became a *tractor trailer*, a *pick up* became a *truck* and a *four wheel drive* car became a *sports utility vehicle, SUV*. A *petrol station* became a *gas station* and there were loonies and toonies and nickels and dimes and quarters as opposed to shillings, sumunis and ndururus. The kind of things I once took for granted were all to be learnt all over again and very quickly! All the same I survived the day.

I spent the next few days reading through every booklet of the many that those smiling ladies that had never forgotten to repeatedly tell me "Welcome to Canada" both in Toronto and in Edmonton had given me. I opened a mail box at the First Edmonton Place and contacted two immigrant serving organizations. I was ready to hit the job market. But I think I was justifiably too optimistic. I spent the next one month preparing and changing and sending resumes that elicited no interest. I followed keenly on all the guidance and leads from my trainers only to realize that what they told me was the general standard but the reality out there appeared to have been quite different. It soon dawned on me that despite having spoken English since my first day of school, I was considered a person with an accent and therefore of questionable academic and professional ability. I called human resource offices of all the banks and insurance companies to no avail.

I did not want to entertain the thought that people were putting me down on account of the color of my skin or the place of my origin. I was literally asked to step away from a job search shop on Jasper Avenue by an Asian lady who happened to be the receptionist. But I thought she did that because of the way I was dressed. It was a cold morning and I was coming from an overnight temporary assignment in steel-toed boots and an all-weather winter jacket with a hood when I noticed the office and decided to walk in. The lady appeared frightened by me and actually asked me to go away because there was nobody to speak to me about jobs in the financial services industry and she did not know when they would report. She confronted me harshly with questions concerning who I was and what I wanted. Although I got offended I did not allow my mind to imagine that the color of my skin had anything to do with her negative attitude. I always believed I was not inhibited from becoming whatever I wanted to become for this was never a subject in Kenya. In any event we had many Asians and *wazungus* in Kenya who were doing extremely well. Some locals could at times complain that their business opportunities were being taken away from them but the general reaction was not to fight the non-Africans. The reaction was the opposite. Some people would mainly seek out whites and the Wa*hindis* as business partners in the hope of developing goodwill in the eyes of their customers. People generally did not have any animosity towards non-Africans. They were perceived as enjoying unique privileges for perhaps having been exposed more to world events and developments. I believed everybody had an equal opportunity if they planned well and worked hard. Even as I began my journey to the developed country that I knew Canada was, I was satisfied that people's attitudes would be above petty tribal and racial animosities. If you pointed out that I was naïve, I would not get offended because this is precisely what I think I was.

In The Thick of Things

I was not only naïve but also too trusting. But I had not had opportunity to see the Chinatown in Edmonton or the Italian colonies in the various cities across North America. I had also not been to Toronto where almost every business on Bathurst Street belonged to the Jews. Kenyans had been friends of the Israelis and I had nothing but respect for the Jews. People in my church had arranged and travelled regularly to Israel and everybody associated the Holy Land with the biblical teachings. My own uncle had travelled with the former Italian ambassador to Kenya in Italy but he never said one negative thing about the Italians. He was always full of praise. Maybe he never understood. I am not sure that he even spoke Italian but since the ambassador's family could do some smattering of Swahili, I can only suspect that my uncle must have lived indoors for the two years that he was in Italy. It may also be that he never quite understood the Italians; the Italians could also be a very nice people. My uncle was also a sojourner and he never wanted to belong anywhere else other than in his original place of birth so the kind of issues that bother some of us today may never have bothered him. We had a huge Italian and Greek community in the North Coast of Kenya and we considered them an important part of our society. Indeed, one of Kenya's assistant ministers for tourism, Mr. Basil Criticos, was of Greek origin and his family owned a significantly large sisal plantation in the Coast province. The Leakey family are a famous Kenyan family and Richard Leakey had once participated actively in a presidential campaign. But that was Kenya. I was now in Canada and my money was running down fast and I knew I had to find a job quickly.

I was ready to do anything decent that paid a wage and in these circumstances, thrashed out a nice looking resume and found a job as a gas station attendant at the West Edmonton Mall. I had seen the ad in a job bank, applied and was hired the same day. In fact the owner came over to my hotel, on his way from his regular job, and we signed the contract at the lobby. I felt extremely lucky and contacted my family the same night to communicate the good news. I lasted eight hours on this job.

There was this young man at the gas station, Jason, whose face kept on twitching. Jason told me he had not been able to complete school because of a health condition and that is why he twitched. Jason was to be my trainer for two hours and I was expected to take over thereafter. He was an extremely friendly white boy and he showed me as much as he could in the shortest time possible. I was also required at the gas station at 5.30 in the morning and without a personal vehicle, I had begun my journey to work that morning with the first bus slightly after 4.30 am. Jason was there and he showed me how to use the dip stick to check the underground supplies and to prepare our office for the first customers. He also gave me a few secrets regarding customer behaviour and how to locate those that were filing gas and how to monitor that they were paying on the closed circuit. Then the owner, Paul, a young man of about twenty six, would call to check my progress every hour while his father, an elderly Filipino gentleman, kept close watch from a tiny back office that had no desk or chair. This was certainly not what brought me to Canada. Certainly this was not the reason that I had acquired master's education in business. I knew this was the wrong place for me. The next time

In The Thick of Things

Paul called, it was towards the end of my shift and he had some interesting news. Since training normally took about four hours and it looked like I was going to need a little bit of a longer duration of training, which was true because I had not used debit cards or mastered all the currency, I was not going to be paid for that day but he was willing to consider extending my training by another four hours the following day.

I knew somebody was being unfair and I told Paul as much and demanded that I got full payment for the eight hours for which I had worked for him. I let him know that I was ready to stay in Canada long enough to receive every pound of my flesh. My bluff worked, and I also think Paul was just a good young guy who never expected people with such high qualifications not to understand the country's currency. It was my fault for not having taken the time to understand the various expectations of the gas station job.

But I also think this is where the disconnect lies between what the Canadian government promulgates, and the reality of immigrating. While the private sector wants one type of employee, the government makes available another kind of employee. I believe there is no point of accepting immigrants from Africa if there were no jobs for them in Canada. Perhaps we should not even take in their refugees if all we really want is to help Africa not to humiliate their people. I believe we can get involved in other more effective ways like providing troops, tactical and financial resources to, for example, end the genocide in places like Darfur, rather than continuing to do business with Khartoum while at the same time pretending to help refugees from that country. I make no apologies for my perception that this is a disguised form of slave trade and human trafficking. Why bring over a doctor who will never be able to practice medicine because of language and race barriers?

But our conscience is soothed when we are perceived to be helping the children of civil wars, as the press appears to love describing young faces from Africa. It is like we have a grudge against the black color, I must lament, for these are just innocent kids and we know there are other more intractable issues. We know how involved we are in those civil wars. We know there are no gun factories in the Democratic Republic of the Congo and we also know that Sierra Leone, Namibia, Angola, Mozambique, DRC and Sudan where the most civil wars have happened are also the most mineral rich countries in the world and in Africa. We know several western corporations and governments have benefited a lot from the resources of these countries. And yet when we show the faces of their children, we call them the children of civil wars that need our mercy.

It comes as no secret that large corporations, owned significantly by many people in North America, take significant oil resources from countries such as Chad where the Sudanese refugees have been pushed. China gets significant oil supplies from Darfur and we continue to wine and dine and do business with the mighty middle kingdom of the east. At the same time we continue to celebrate the ending of slave trade by Wilberforce 500 years ago! We may fool ourselves sometimes but I think it is criminal when we do it all the time. I have some special respect for Mayor David Miller of Toronto. When a 15 year old black boy was gunned down by some gang

In The Thick of Things

from the corridors of his school, Mayor Miller confessed that he could not face the boy's parents in the eyes and tell them that what happened would not happen again, because he felt the federal government had not done enough to protect certain members of the Canadian community. Whether Mr. Miller had done enough himself as the mayor of the most violent city in Canada is a different story altogether. What matters to me is his acknowledgement and acceptance that there were important issues that we were capable of dealing with but which we had chosen not to.

Without a job, but with a small taste of the market, I called randomly and I got a furnished bachelor suite in the slum area of Edmonton on 97 Street which was the only place where four hundred dollars could find an apartment. The room looked nice and clean, with a stove and a fridge, the kind of amenities land lords never provided in Kenya. Moreover, David, my care taker, also provided me with a small single bed with some two bed sheets and a blanket. These were all the things that I ever needed in a house. My plan now, that I had a home, was to go to those work-ready shops, and there was one right in my neighbourhood, and to do menial jobs during the day, and spend the evenings in a cybercafé on Jasper Avenue in town where they provided internet services, looking for proper jobs. And many 'true' Canadians, which seemed to mean white Canadian, congratulated me for being realistic. It had not yet dawned on me that indeed this is what was expected of me and this is the reason why the embassy does not get too involved in determining whether one had all that was needed to find work within the shortest time possible because there is always work in Canada. What there isn't in Canada is the right kind of work for everybody. I certainly had not yet heard or figured out what the concepts of one manager and four Indians meant. I was an Indian who aspired to become a manager, and once an Indian always an Indian!

My plan worked like clockwork on the first day. I got a job in a factory warehouse under construction. Since the construction machines could not reach every nook and cranny of the building, my job was to rake and level the dirt and the soil around the tight corners. It was also my job to pump down the soil onto the ground with a machine that threatened to tear away my biceps. I could not sleep that evening. I was extremely tired and exhausted. Nevertheless, I still walked downtown and spent the night and money preparing and sending resumes just as I had planned.

The following day started with a heavy blistering snowfall. I believed I could find my directions to the place I had worked the previous day but I completely got lost. You see they never tell you the name of the company you work for when they hire you in those job-ready places. They give you the name of the supervisor for the day and they may also drop you off at the work site as had happened with me. My supervisor had liked my work habit and I had been asked to report the following day, but I had forgotten to take the address of the work site. So when the bus dropped me off at the terminus that happened to have been the end of the route, I got lost and wandered aimlessly for hours until finally after asking anybody I could find I located my place of work. It was nearly mid-day. I felt sleepy, exhausted, mentally tortured, physically weak and generally incapable of heavy manual labour. I attempted work for one hour but then I was overcome and for the second time since arriving in Canada I tendered my resignation. Dejected and hungry I went looking for transport back to 97th Street.

I slept for two days straight, dazed as to what madness brought me over to this place that appeared offended by my very presence. I finally woke up with a cracking headache and to my worst fears after a few tests at the Queen Victoria Hospital, my cancer was confirmed to have recurred.

Despite the apparent rejection, I was still satisfied that I had not yet exhausted every available opportunity. I embarked on a door to door job search in addition to the internet efforts. I finally landed a job as a security guard with Signature Group. I worked as one of the security guards for Oxford Bell Tower, the then tallest building in Edmonton. The job entailed manning the security desk and locking down the elevators after hours. I was also required to inspect, on an hourly basis, the three underground parking basements and each one of the thirty six floors. I think security guards are a very responsible underpaid bunch. For eight dollars on the hour, I had the keys to each one of the rooms of this tower including the boiler rooms and all the offices. I would check every nook and cranny to ensure nobody was hiding in some corners of an office on the 33rd, 10th or 22nd floors. I would at times find myself in awkward situations where I would open some door to a private office and find people in compromising positions. I would apologise and quickly leave them to their not so official businesses. And I think everybody also understood that the security guard meant no harm. They would later pass by downstairs and exchange pleasant smiles with me and pretend that I had not seen anything. It was like a silent bond. It was like telling me, Peter we trust you and that is why you are our security guard. We expect you to honour the privileges of your office. Just as they do in banking. As a banker, I learnt many years ago that the greatest asset of any bank is the confidentiality of customer information that translates into reputation capital. In the event a financial institution lost this capital, public confidence wanes and nobody can any longer invest their deposits with such a financial institution. I did my job with zeal and dignity and quickly established good rapport with my colleagues.

I was later transferred to Alberta College where I worked with Jody, a First Nations lady, who complained all the time. Jody was especially concerned about writing reports for we were required to make statements and reports concerning any untoward activities happening during our shifts. A lot of drunks would come looking for shelter and it was my responsibility to scare them away from the building. It was also my duty to ensure there were no break-ins and petty thefts that were so frequent at Alberta College, an institutions that had many activities including night studies for immigrant and local young adults who came to upgrade their high school qualifications. There were also various music festivals including those organised by the Kiwanis group, pronounced Kuwannas. The Kiwanis group would join me in manning the security desk for they wanted to directly usher in their members.

In The Thick of Things

I was in one of these Kiwanis activities that I met my friend Roy Bird, a very open minded and outgoing special constable of the Royal Canadian Mounted Police. Perhaps I have a special place for cops because my late father used to be one and I know I feared and respected my dad. Or perhaps it was just the natural affinity of characters. In the next few days, Roy invited me to visit with him and with his girlfriend and the both of them offered to show me Canada. On one weekend, at no cost to me, we travelled all the way west to the Rocky Mountains and this was my first really good experience about my new country. Mr. Bird encouraged me not to give up on my job search and I hit the job market again. My faith in the country was reignited.

In the next few weeks through the help of another very outgoing and friendly gentleman, Mr. Mike Brover, a Jewish gentleman who once worked as a disc jockey and whose wife was a community manager for a credit union, I managed to secure an interview with the credit union for a part-time position as a teller. Within the same month I also managed to secure another interview for a commercial account manager position with one of the chartered banks in Edmonton. Things looked quite promising that February. While matters progressed quite slowly at chartered bank, I was finally able to join the credit union on May 4th 2003 at an hourly rate of \$10.26 for 21 hours a week, just slightly more than what my grade 10 son is working for this summer. I could hardly meet my monthly bills and had therefore to go moonlighting at Wal-Mart mixing paints for another four hours at \$8.00 per hour each evening.

After several conversations and subsequent interviews, I was finally offered a more permanent position as a bank teller by chartered bank in November 2003, ten months from the time we began our initial conversations. And the job was after all for a completely different position from the commercial manager position I had originally applied for. In the next nine months, I was gradually promoted to become a commercial credit officer in commercial banking reporting to six commercial account managers. Unfortunately, by this time, I had already developed a deep sense that the colour of my skin and place of origin were significant factors in determining my career progress not only in that bank but anywhere else in Canada. I had also now come to learn about the treatment of Canadian Aboriginals and the history of colonialism. Not only was I more professionally and academic qualified, I also had more work experience than most of the account managers that I was then working for. A gnawing sense of injustice lingered in my heart despite the promotions that I am sure my friend and boss the VP for human resources must have ensured happen. The VP for HR had struggled without success for ten months to find a senior commercial area manager who could take me into his staff in a bank that was adding a new branch almost on a quarterly basis on account of the boom in western Canada where their niche is. He had to finally take me in as a bank teller.

When the opportunity for a commercial account manager position with another came along, I did not feel any loyalty to my employer and immediately left. This, I think, was the beginning of the end of my banking career in Canada.

"Peter you are so intelligent. What I like about you is that you not only point out problems but you also come up with practical solutions", my hiring manager would occasionally praise me. It was the most enjoyable three months in my career since coming to Canada. Not only was I working in a managerial position, in the banking industry in Canada, but I also had a manager who appreciated my maturity and experience. She would speak to people about me with a lot of pride in her tone and I knew I had made a good decision to come over to this bank. Meantime she also had to put up spirited battles with several offices on my behalf to facilitate my training opportunities. I would at times find her frustrated that everybody she spoke to appeared to have a ready negative response for whatever she asked for me. In fact, she had not managed to find a specific desk for me in the three months; I had been rotated to more than five offices wherever somebody was on vacation. This lady, unfortunately, was several months pregnant and soon left for maternity leave.

After my guardian angel left my training was immediately brought to a crashing end. I was immediately relocated to my work location in a small town of seven thousand where the Bank's branch had been without a commercial manager for more than a year. This meant that I had nobody to mentor me on my work site as is the practice in that bank. My new area manager was four hours away and when we met for the first time, upon introductions his first question was whether I was really sure that this was the job that I wanted. It appeared never to matter to him how well I did my job or the amount of business that I brought to the bank. He desperately wanted me out. In each of the five times I worked for this gentleman, there was always something about alternative job offers for me. "Peter you are so qualified and this town will be a silo for you. It does not matter how well you work for me. How about going to work in corporate finance in Calgary? Would you like me to help you find a job there?" Once I said yes, only to later receive feedback that the position had already been filled. Then he turned to humiliating me. I remember one week when he was meant to come visiting my area. He was to come to my branch on a Thursday. I had complained to him that a branch staff had acted rudely towards me. He nevertheless summoned me to see him at 8.00 on a Tuesday morning in his branch, four hours away and I therefore had to leave home at 5.00am in order that I could be on time. Despite my pleas he was not ready to wait another two days when we would discuss the matter when he was in town. In his words, he wanted to teach me Canadian culture, whatever it was meant to be, for when we finally met, we never really discussed anything. He had no good reason for calling me over. But he was happy that I had obeyed. Perhaps he was just daring me to disobey. I have never found greatness in disobedience and there was no way I could have refused to go.

The next time I was invited apparently for an account manager's breakfast in his city, I got rudely shocked to realize that after several hours on the highway the breakfast had only been meant for me, himself and the Vice President of the region, who had travelled the previous night and spent the night in that city only so that they could meet with me. Besides having the breakfast, the only question I was asked was whether there was enough business in my town. And as I lingered on in that city attending to more meetings with my boss, the VP drove out to my branch in my absence. It was quite clear my presence was causing too much concern to the executive. No wonder there were no other black commercial account managers in the whole region. My probationary period was extended at 5.00pm for another 90 days on the last day of the six months. The 90 days of grace was also considered too long and I was dismissed at 8.00am on March 31st 2005. I was told I was not a good fit. My very presence appeared to have been a great eyesore to my management. If this is what is called racism, then I think the people who practice it lead very difficult and painful lives. I think it is a life of wishful thinking of what they would want to see the world look like instead of celebrating our diversity, embracing our subtle differences and what we can achieve together. This management appeared to have gone to great lengths to find good reasons to get rid of me despite the fact that I was still on probation and they could have simply sent me away which they in any event finally did. But I now know why they were being that cautious because my Alberta experience was not the last time I worked for that bank. I also later worked for them in Toronto.

My recent letter to the Canadian Human Rights Commission summarizes my subsequent experience. The Commission has acknowledged my letter and like me they also think the bank has violated some aspects of the law and I am now awaiting subsequent developments.

"Peter Mwangi – The Bank"

I have reasonable grounds for believing that I have been discriminated against. I declare that the following is true to the best of my knowledge.

My name is Peter Mwangi and my complaint is against the bank. I am a black man in his forties and immigrated to Canada from Africa.

I am a fully qualified financial professional. I have had 18 years banking experience including a stint as one of the executives for a commercial bank. I have reason to believe that I was subjected to discrimination and harassment on account of the colour of my skin, age, race, high level qualifications, and the place of my origin.

I joined the bank for the first time in August 2004 as an Account Manager for a small town in Alberta on a career progression from another chartered Bank. My hiring manager went on maternity leave three months after my hire half-way through my training before being posted to my branch. Reporting line for my branch was changed from one centre to another and my training curtailed. I reported to my branch effective November 01, 2004. My new area manager, made junior job offers to me on two of the four occasions that we met. His request on our first meeting was that I "step back so that I could move forward". Harassment continued despite the fact that I was exceeding set business goals and customer feedback was positive. My services were terminated on March 31, 2005. The Bank's response to my complaint through the Director of Employee Relations was that the decision to terminate my services was the right one.

I found a job once again with the Bank on April 24th 2006 reporting to Mrs. X, one of two senior team leaders. Mrs X reported to M/S Y, the senior manager. M/S Y in turn reported to Mr., the Vice President responsible for the Business segment in Canada.

I was the only black African. I was also one of eight new employees. The other employees came from within the personal banking side of the business on promotion. Indeed one of them had been a team leader in Personal Banking. The Bank's policy requires that all commercial account managers undergo a rigorous six to nine months training co-ordinated by the Bank's Institute for Financial Learning (IFL), credit risk management and the vice-president of the department. I was denied this training opportunity, an unusual exception to Bank policy. Also, in order to complete a Commercial Credit Application, the set up of the Bank's computer system is such that one must have the capacity to complete a Personal Credit Application. The other employees, including the new ones, on account of their experience in personal lending had this capacity. I did not have this ability.

During training, employees alternate between the IFL and the office. While in the office they help their allocated mentors complete credit applications with the work output being the responsibility of the mentor. My case was special. While I had a mentor, Mr. RB allocated to me, my work output was my responsibility. I was also told that my training would be accelerated for completion in three months when I would be sent to credit risk management for assessment and confirmation of my credit skills. I was restricted to seeking help from only Mr. RB or Mrs. X.

Reporting times were staggered such that there were always people in the office between 7.00am and 8.00pm, Monday to Friday. At first I used to report as early as 7.00 am in the hope of finding some self-training from the Bank's computer system. I was instructed not to report before RB was in the office. I was also restricted from working late in *the evenings. RB would ask me to come to the office, say at 9.00 the following morning. He would however not show up until 11.00 and then after only about 10 or so minutes he would go away for an hour of private gym training to improve his football abilities. He would then go for lunch and then either work late or surprisingly get excused to go home early. This completely confused my training efforts.*

I soon realized that Mr. RB was not ready to train me and he confessed this to me. He would frequently amuse the office with tasteless jokes made very loudly for all to hear with comments such as "Mr. Mwangi our meeting is to start in the next two minutes. Are you still operating on African time? Mr. Mwangi, in your view do credit applications at our bank meet Kenyan credit standards?" Most of my colleagues were in the same age, career and education bracket with RB would give me a lot of trouble with my credit applications with his popular comments made for all to hear that all he was doing was trying to "humble down MBA- type applications down to our grass roots level". He would send them back and forth to me for reasons such as the choice of numbering of items instead of bullets and where there were bullets he would re-change them back to numbering and back again to bullets. Talk in the office was that I was the new guy in the "penalty box". Everybody expected that it was only a matter of time before I was fired. RB once told me he was unhappy that Mrs. X was making him do her dirty laundry.

I made a decision early on to whenever possible direct my applications to X. I received a lot of praise from X throughout May and June.

The only incident was in June when the VP joined our team for a lunch outing. He sat directly in front of me and as conversation ranged about vacations and such, Mr. Z all

In The Thick of Things

of a sudden posed the question "Peter, do you people go on vacation?" I was surprised by the words "you people". Later, the following day, X told me that the VP believed that I did not understand English well enough to work in a call centre and he had asked Y to look into it. X was on vacation in the second and third week of July 2006.

During X's absence, RB became extremely abusive, hostile and unfriendly. I reported to the other Senior Team Leader, Mr. LK, who dealt with my concerns to my entire satisfaction. Upon the return of X however, she gave me a letter on July 28, 2006 that among other things stated that "Peter has shown a willingness to provide excellent customer service. Peter gets along with his team mates. He participates with discussions during team meetings and has some valuable input". It also stated "Peter has been assigned a mentor who is seasoned and a high performing team member. It appears Peter's past work experience and exposure may not be applicable to the grass roots IB lending".

Also on 28th July, instead of being sent to credit risk management for assessment of my skills as promised upon hire, Mrs. X allocated me business targets for a weekly $35,000 worth of new business. Please note that the other new employees did not have business targets on this date. In fact by September 16th I was at 164% of my annual target. On Sunday September 24th, I completed an application for $700,000 worth of new business that had I been permitted to record it would have pushed my year-to-date accomplishment to 323%.

Mentoring was also ended on July 28th 2006. Henceforth, X compiled a list of anything on my credit applications that she did not agree with irrespective of whether I had a reason for it. Credit reports are subjective and are based on interpretation. Discussions are always part of the credit approval process. In addition, X would regularly visit my pod, sit on the small space on my desk in the full view of all my colleagues and make comments such as "this is a fast paced work environment different from what you may have experienced in Africa". Mrs. X being a motherly figure with 33 years experience, I found her abrupt change in her style of management extremely offending and frightening. Specifically, on August 11, 2006, I requested her, and I was crying in deep humiliation, that we go into the coaching room because I was getting very embarrassed. This request became the ground for my first warning letter on August 22, 2006. I sought the help of Y, who indicated that she had full faith in X. On this date also I was given a new training schedule indicating that my training in the same mode of delivery was to re-start for re-assessment in January 2007. I received a second letter on September 08, 2006 listing apparent credit mistakes that according to Mrs. X reflected deviations. Meantime my colleagues were still on training.

My services were terminated at 5.00 pm on September 28, 2006. I believe strongly that the Bank through its management has a discriminating and racist policy against qualified black men in an effort to stop them from ever getting to senior management positions in that Bank.

I have not been able to find alternative work as my credibility has been destroyed and potential employers once they learn that I have been fired have chosen not to progress with my candidacy. I have justifiable fear that I may never again be able to benefit from many years of dedicated work effort, academic and professional pursuits. I am seeking help in obtaining reasonable and fair compensation for damages for a destroyed career that any person in the financial services industry in Canada with my level of qualifications and experience would receive. I am also seeking special damages *for pain and anguish that I have suffered since March 2005. I also seek compensation for lost income over the last eight months that I have been without work. Thank you."*

Despite the many settling down troubles that I have faced since coming over, I have carried on in the conviction that I have not yet exhausted all available avenues. I have continued to allow my mind to imagine that there are still some good people remaining and have earnestly sought the friendship of as many people from as many backgrounds and races as possible. So far, unfortunately, I have continued to be confronted with the ugly reality and evidence that whereas there are so many very nice people at the individual level, and I can name a few of such extremely well adjusted people, there seems to be too much pressure from a small group that is extremely influential. I think it is just like it is with special groups in politics where a whole society seems to care so much and to be driven by the needs of a small special interest group. It is similar in mob justice, where a group of otherwise very good people all of a sudden find themselves involved in some very abysmal activities.

I have looked closely and reviewed the various places where I have worked. Most executives and management at the Edmonton Bank appeared to have some connection to Germany. Most employees would either have a spouse, a friend or some kind of heritage with Germany. Community group leaders at the credit union appeared to have been selected on the basis of their association with tribal enclaves, for example, the Hindu community, the Jewish community, the Iranian community and such. As I frantically searched for work, I had the opportunity to arrange interviews with most of the leaders of the chartered banks in Edmonton. Most of them were of a proud British heritage. One time received a response from a certain human resources executive in Calgary that I could not be hired by his bank. I pursued for reasons but I was left to draw my own conclusions.

Faced with these realities, as an independent first generation Canadian from Africa, you all of a sudden find yourself in an extremely cold place. And the weather in Edmonton is also very cold, so this becomes some kind of a double whammy, and this is where I first landed on the last day of January 2003.

Few people know Canada well. I did not know it so well either for more than three years. It is an extremely huge country. I drove from Alberta, in a small town called Drumheller, where there are caricatures of dinosaurs at the corner of every street and in front of every commercial building. There are businesses upon businesses that thrive on dinosaur images. The local lingo is intertwined with words like tyrannosaurus rex, velociraptors, hadrosaur and words with such complex pronunciation. Some of the creatures are so huge you trace town properties by looking at the skyline for the jutting images of these weird carvings of animals that the paleontologists and archeologists that roam this south eastern corner of Alberta claim to have existed several million years ago. Why, when they died, they all chose to bring their bones and concentrate them after all these years at this shallow river bed of the Red Deer River for the scientists to find them beats my unscientific mind. But that is neither here nor there.

My journey begun on a Friday afternoon and I was not in Toronto until Mid-night on Sunday after a grueling sixty hours on the highway. I drove through the cities of Medicine Hat in Alberta, Regina in Saskatchewan, Winnipeg in Manitoba, Kenora, Thunder Bay, Salt St.

In The Thick of Things

Marie, and Sudbury in Ontario before wrapping up my safari in Toronto. What I can tell you today is that if you have not yet driven through that route that you please don't try. My car had a manual transmission engine because this is what I was used to in Kenya and I did not want to learn how to drive on the "right" side of the road while also re-learning how to drive, for driver licenses in Canada are recognized on a Province- by -Province basis let alone recognition of licenses from Africa. I can assure you that covering three thousand kilometers without a co-driver is a challenging affair and requires that you have a pretty determined soul. I did it!

We have a population of thirty three million in Canada, the same number as Kenya's. There is no reason that anybody should suffer want in this country. Even if there were no service jobs and we did not have any factories whatsoever, and we all decided to rear Moose, we would have enough Moose to feed the world. Each male, female and child would have their ten or more Moose to provide meat and hide to the rest of the world. And Canada would still not be full.

But when you have too much you naturally relax. Is it not strange that so many people in this great nation still want to identify with the small enclaves from where their great grandparents hailed? Imagine how people in continental Europe are proud of being Greek, Cypriot, Italian, Danish etc. The Arabs and the Africans are also proud of being Lebanese, Rwandans, and other nationalities. And when we are in Canada we feel proud to identify with these tiny places of our ancestors. Granted, we have to love our motherlands but I think if we were to come off this infatuation and focused on making the best of this mighty strong jewel of the north with all its endowments, we would never have to linger on where we hailed. Look at the Americans and their American dream. Three hundred million odd congregated in one small place in relative terms and yet their gross domestic product is more than ten times ours. Why? Were we born after them? What has happened in all these four hundred years since the first settlers came to these shores? Are we also like Kenyan politicians who, at least during my days in that country, behaved as if they were about to move to some other countries?

The little history I have read about Canada tells me that when the first governments realized that they needed more people to settle in this country, they encouraged people to come over based on those peoples' skin color and the places of their origin while at the same time pushing away the original inhabitants, the First Nations people. When you do things that way, you plant a sickness, a cancer of entitlement on the one hand and simmering discontent on the other hand. You introduce a culture of us versus them. And the so called "us' is a bunch of strangers united by nothing more than the shades of their skin, the length of their limbs and the color of their hair. This is the lowest that any human being can ever go to. And yet we have such a beautiful national anthem.

Generations gained from nepotism, unwarranted favors and largesse dolled out disproportionately for free at the expense of the mutual good for all. The aboriginals are not about to go anywhere. They are human beings that appreciate positive deeds and no wonder have worked out all these agreements with successive Canadian governments. Why not assimilate them into the centre of things and invite them unconditionally to participate in the dream Canada? Why not do the same for everybody?

In The Thick of Things

Of course I understand we are a capitalist nation and there are no free lunches. But we have so much and we are so intelligent not to plunder what we have. I am also not blind and I dare not speculate that the United States is a paradise for I know it is not for I have never seen so many beggars in one place as I saw the other day when I visited Boston and Cambridge in Massachusetts. There is some human being with a begging bowl at every corner of each street in these small cities of the US. Some are so ingenious they pretend to be selling "Panhandling Times" as the morning newspapers. So naturally when you go to buy, you realize it is the only one the guy has and in fact it is actually not a newspaper but a poster meant to camouflage the activity which I think is illegal in those cities because it makes the billionaires uncomfortable. And when I caught a cold while in the hospital where my son had undergone surgery and I went to the ICIU in the fear that I would spread flu to the patients in the wards, they sent me a bill of USD.2000. Ridiculous! Americans are dying from fevers and colds because their medical system is tailored towards the rich and famous. The unfortunate thing is that these poor souls were born and brought up in the cities, unlike my grandpa in Africa who would have taught them how to become ninety six years old without ever having gone to hospital. In fact I even at times imagine that had it not been for his bull that beat him up when he was still advanced in age, my grandpa could as well be still alive. But I am talking about the United States and Canada not about some African natives who never went to hospitals. They may as well have had tails. We beat the Americans hands down when it comes to our medical system and the cleanliness of our cities here in Canada. But life is not just about hospitals and drugs and dying. We need our pride of place as a people and we have resources that are unparalleled by nobody else, maybe Russia. But the Russians have had their limiting issues as well and they do not speak English so they lack in a major way; the people that come from far and wide to bless our heritage.

I remember before I got exhausted with being shafted and I was actively looking for work in Toronto, I went and met several people who proudly proclaimed that in Canada, you do not find a job because of what you know but rather because of who you know. This is official nepotism. I have been to countless public offices where husband and wife, parents and their children and brothers and sisters work in the same offices. Surely, how can justice and fairness and/or its appearance be served by such practices. These practices were discouraged and discontinued in many places at least fifteen years ago in Europe and in Africa.

Since there are so many opportunities for everybody in Canada why have relatives giving negative blessings to offices? How do we tell those about us that we are professional if this is what they see?" Is it a wonder then that the culture of aligning with our ancestral enclaves and technically remaining tribesmen, just like the Hottentots in Timbuktu, the Dinka in Southern Sudan and the Maasai in the jungles of Africa are?. How different are we from the tourist guide tribes in the slopes of Mt. Everest and the Himalayas? How can we possibly be expected to fully exploit the resources at our disposal? I think the greatest downside that we suffer is failing to understand the most important thing in a human beings life. I think this thing is seeing that those that neighbor us are happy for being with us. How would you like to live in a sprawling slum? Why do you hate it? Why do you want to go away? How about changing this place and making it a small paradise? And this is why I am angry with myself. I strongly believed in this line of thinking many years ago. I called the opposite, the public toilet syndrome, where one person messes the loo and since it is public, the next person comes and dumps their stuff even nearer the door rather taking responsibility and cleaning up the mess lack of payment notwithstanding. We are capable of doing so much good. But I drifted away from where I had the greatest opportunity to achieve this human fulfillment. This is why I think the Americans in Boston and Massachusetts with so many desperate about are less happy than the proud Maasai in the Maasai Mara and the Serengeti animal reserves in East Africa because they walk with their *chukkas* floating about proudly notwithstanding their bare bottoms. A millionaire who lives in a graveyard is indeed the poorest soul the world ever had. So, Canada please wake up. Empower your sons and daughters so that they do not shame you. Do not try to hide with a blade of grass. Everybody is seeing your nakedness. You are able but you refuse to play your role.

Chapter Seven

My Faith, My Religion, My Journey

I do not just want to say that life has been unfair to me because these words would not be strong enough to account for the humiliation and the pain that has been meted out against my grandpa, my father, my mother and me. I would only be complaining because it would not have been me on the benefiting side. I would be adopting the victim mentality that many people may think this is a sensible mentality to adopt when you are in my circumstances. For starters none of my relatives were white in colonial Kenya so they were all on the receiving end as natives. Then my grandpa went to Europe and Asia risking limb and life to win wars for a kingdom that did not recognize him as a human being, for he had no pay or pension and died a native, not a celebrated war veteran. My two grandmas died when both my parents were young. The young kids got subjected to untold suffering at an early age. Then both my parents and I lived under tyranny when Kenya became free from colonial exploitation.

In The Thick of Things

As if the foregoing was not enough, pain followed me over when I immigrated to a white man's country in the hope that I would find justice out there only to realize that the people in the streets were perhaps not just seeing another human being but rather associated me with events of a far away continent that I had nothing to do with. I was fired from jobs with little consideration and despite all the qualifications that I thought I had. I was quickly relegated to the lowest ranks of my society and became nothing more than just another jobless black man. The immediate reaction and I have indeed at times felt this way, is to hate the world and coil myself into some corner and wait for my days just as my grandpa did, or worse, go the route of my father who was younger and had less patience. I refuse to follow either route. I have the right to be here! All I crave for is to use the faculties that the almighty God gave me to eke out a living and to contribute to the welfare of our parent. If I have to do this in the form of a protest note then let it be so.

The Bible story tells us how the Jews, the sons of David, suffered while in Egypt and we know their suffering because they expressed it. I love some of the lyrics of the song *By the rivers of Babylon* that goes something like *"By the rivers of Babylon, where we sat down, and there we wept when we remembered Zion. When the river carried us away to captivity---how shall we sing the Lord's praise in a strange land---?* Yes indeed, how shall we sing the Lord's praise in a strange land? Who at the Canadian embassies around the world tells the independent immigrants that their resumes are not good enough and they would have to spend months and years being shown how to prepare resumes? Who tells senior bankers, engineers and doctors that they would be needed to go back to school for years before their new society can accept their qualifications after the rigor and the waiting in the immigration process?

If I were to define who I was, I would perhaps describe myself as a highly resilient human being, proficient in the field of business and finance, possessing a questioning, inquisitive mind, kind, inwardly confident, rather bold, widely traveled, determined, highly analytical, sincere, dependable, curious but cautious and open-minded. I do not boast for any of these qualities. I do not own them. They just came to me while I was a sojourner. But they are good qualities for the purpose because they enable me to share my story without fear, without hesitation and without bile.

I think I have also been on a rather interesting journey. It is not over yet, so I am, quite interestingly, awaiting developments in the next few years. I believe, at the moment, I am in the middle of a new watershed, a new beginning, just like all the other beginnings before the next one. I dare say that my life has only been a journey and there has neither been fulfillment nor loss. It has only been a journey albeit a rather painful one. All that really matters to me now is how I have dealt with the obstacles and the vanities that I have encountered along the way. And this has given me a sense of wanting to be here longer. At least to be a leading light to those who depend on me so that they may not have to make the same mistakes that I may have made on my journey. I also hope to be able to share my experiences with those others who may be interested and therefore there is value

In The Thick of Things

in my being on this journey a little longer for my sake and for the sake of others.

I have nobody to quote from and I do not know whether what I say will be considered wise or foolish. It is for others to decide. All the wise quotes were given to us by those that were on this journey before us. They played their part and then departed. We also have our part to play. Must we also defer our experiences to those of others who were on the same journey so that we are seen to abide by this convention?

My path has been through many twists and turns, ups and downs, and I have finally come to the categorical conclusion that I have a story that needs to be shared for whatever it is worth. I use the word categorical because I started toying with the idea of writing this story of my life ten years ago but was then too busy with my job at the bank in Nairobi to find the time. Life was good but I still knew I was not settled. I knew I was soon going to retire from that job and do something else, although I was only thirty years old and had enjoyed several promotions in the ten years that I had worked for that bank. My gross salary had increased from $400 per year to $60000 within this period. I had also been promoted several times from an entry level clerical job to become one of the four global corporate account managers for that bank. I was responsible for the restructuring of the largest book of non-performing debts of the company in order to restore the Bank's credit quality following a period of poor lending decisions by the company's management. Yet, I was feeling a strong desire to go out, complete a graduate degree, set up my own business and become truly free and independent. I felt caged, staved off action and I think some things don't change until you do what you must do. I wanted to be able to tell a story but I could not for several reasons, but the main obstacle was me.

I wanted to wait a little longer. I was still uncertain about my position on a number of issues that I felt needed more in-depth investigation. I was not entirely confident about my faith, my education, parental experience, travels, wealth or lack thereof, socio-political experience, and professional experience including international exposure. I felt my ideas were half-through formed and that they needed more tuning up before I could confidently and authoritatively tell my story. But then this was ten years ago. I was back in Africa and had only traveled to a few cities mainly in Africa.

Altogether, I have now traveled, lived or worked in the following places: Toronto, Drumheller, Edmonton, Kerugoya, Othaya, Nairobi, Nakuru, Mombasa, London, Manchester, Wales, Little Rock, Dallas-Forthworth, Harare, Searcy, Harare, Boston, Cambridge, Mazvikadei, Chicago, New York, Chimanimani, Kihuri, Ihuririo, Kagaya, Calgary, Red Deer, Winnipeg, Regina, Banff, Bangor, Thika, Nanyuki, Ol'Kalau and several other places. I consider myself well traveled.

Besides my university research project on the methods of dealing with non-performing debts in the banking industry in Kenya in 2001 and an industry survey on the cement industry ten years before then, the closest I came to writing anything public was in 2001/2002 when I published *Business Trumpet*, a quarterly business journal that I used to educate the public and to promote my investment consultancy when I formed a consulting

In The Thick of Things

company in Central Kenya. Had I had more of these exposures, I think by now I would have become a household name. And people might have paid more attention if I ever came along with a more serious message for I think this one is.

I have had the opportunity to work for and in various capacities in commercial account manager positions for a several banks in Canada and overseas. I was a corporate manager responsible for large corporations in East Africa including Colgate Palmolive, Cussons, Unga Group, Magadi Soda, Delmonte and Smith Kline Beecham among several others. I placed several companies under receivership and recovered substantial amounts of debt. I have also worked as a manager responsible for credit risk management for a banking corporation and as a Risk Analyst in Toronto. I have had the chance to work as a senior credit officer for an Edmonton bank and as a bank teller for a credit union in Edmonton. I was the security guard, I mean the night watchman, for Alberta College and for the Oxford Bell Tower in Edmonton when I worked for some security guard company in that city. I have told you that I worked in a gas station and as a building construction factory hand where I raked dirt around circular corners in Edmonton. Beyond all this, I owned Maria M. Body Care Products and Marigiti Café jointly with my wife, Mary.

I purchased land, planned, drew the sketches, sourced funding and all the required materials, supervised the digging of a water well, the latrine and compost pits, planting of trees, cultivation, planting and weeding of the land, and the construction of a three bedroomed concrete house on our land in Kerugoya, Kenya. Have I done something familiar to what you have done, my dear reader? Have we worked together somewhere? I think I have had a most unique opportunity to work in many fields and in many places giving me valuable experience and a very different perspective about jobs and people's attitudes towards work and career success.

I have voluntarily tendered resignations from six bad jobs and I have been fired from three, the latter within the last two years. I have been promoted eight times and my annual salary has oscillated between $400 and $60000 and anywhere else in between with several break-outs on the lower side during periods of no work. I have been to unemployment insurance and have done several survival jobs. I have also had the opportunity to make presentations to boards of directors and to conduct a country visit of the global executive directors of a global bank with my customers and to participate in a small team that prepared all the banking procedures of that bank before a level three business process re-engineering.

I was admitted to pursue PhD studies by the University of Wales in 2002 but could not take on my position due to lack of scholarship and funding in Africa. I completed MBA studies in July 2001 by distance learning. I was selected and awarded a $40,000 scholarship for overseas training in a post –graduate certificate in business and subsequently a $20000 MBA grant to study at the same university by my employer between 1993 and 2001.I enjoyed great financial comfort and travel during and after the time of my studies. I am sure there are many readers who will readily identify with this sweet experience. I paid off my loans including my mortgage and supported friends and family in significant ways.

In The Thick of Things

By the way, circumstances forced me to quit school while doing my 'A' level studies at the age of nineteen. I wanted to become a medical doctor. The money to take me to school had been borrowed against my wish, on the security of the only cow my family had and this at a time when my mother was very sick and also at a time when Kenya was experiencing great famine. All my seven brothers and sisters, except my older sister, were dependent on this cow's milk. I went to school feeling very guilty. If I could not help them, I could at least help myself by not being an extra burden for the family. Education was however extremely important to me and to the family so I reluctantly took up my place at Kagumo high school, one of the top national schools for 'A' level education for the boys who had excelled in the general high school examinations. I stayed in Kagumo for three months and then decided to walk home, a good fifty kilometers, driven by a curiosity to inquire on the welfare of my family. What I found there was dire. I left Kagumo the following Monday, returned the money and went out on an aggressive job hunt all over the country. After all I was now an adult. I was eighteen years old, two months shy of my nineteenth birthday. Ultimately, I found a job with Standard Chartered Bank and did all my studying while I worked for that Bank. I married early at an age of twenty two and we were blessed with our two sons in 1987 and in 1992. I did my 'A' levels in 1987, stage 1 of the Chartered Institute of bankers between 1985 and 1986, and an international diploma in banking between 1988 and 1992. I was sponsored for a post-graduate certificate in business by my bank in 1993 and completed an MBA degree in 2001. I have done the mutual funds course in Canada and have passed Chartered Financial Analyst exams in January 2007. I continue to pursue more knowledge and to support my family. When I have no money to give them, I give them encouragement and guidance and most of my presence and care. I think I have had some valiant academic and life experience that is worth sharing.

And as if the foregoing was not enough, I have previously been diagnosed with a pituitary adenoma, a cancer in the brain that is only treatable through surgery. I have traveled the globe searching for a cure and at one time had to bid my young family goodbye as we made my own funeral arrangements. Miraculously, I somehow recovered without surgery and the doctor that I saw last thought it was all a hoax. Despite all the previous MRIs and surgeons who were eager to operate, my last doctor thought I was never actually sick and I should not have been on any medication. I do not entirely agree with him but since I am sickness free why should I sweat the small bad stuff. I hope nobody will have to go through this kind of experience. However, if this is your cup, how much choice do you really have?

Mary and I are proud parents of Gerald and Isaiah. I enjoy the company of my wife Mary. This does not however mean that we do not have our quarrels. We do, however, we avoid unnecessary arguments about money or lack of it, because we know that people are as poor or as wealthy as they want to be. We have since learnt not to rub in the bad stuff as and when it happens.

For many years I admired my mother's kind of faith. That sweet unquestioning, unfailing, eternal love for the word of God that has always been preached to me since

In The Thick of Things

I was young and I have in turn earnestly sought after it. Many times I have convinced myself that I have found an answer and yet at others times I have felt lost and confused. But Nyayo was also a born again Christian and a dangerous crook, I dare say, for he plunged the resources of a nation, willfully.

The more I age also and have had the chance to travel and to interact more with the world, my admiration for my mother's kind of faith has wavered and where there once was admiration, I have felt pity and frustration. I have felt frustrated by not only the embarrassment of knowing that my own mother has lived all her life in this unquestioning, unreasoning way but also by the realization that I have not previously been able to connect all these dots. I have felt even more frustrated by the realization that even as I connect these dots there is not much that I can do to effect any meaningful change in the life of my mother, or even worse, in the life of my father who left this world so young and so long ago. How could, I now find myself asking, a fourteen year old illiterate Kikuyu girl in nineteen forty eight Kenya, understand and fully accept some foreign religion? She never read a Bible because she did not know how to read and she never asked any questions because she would not have known what questions to ask. This child was just looking for love, help and sympathy and that is what she got from her neighbors' daughters and from her mother's age mate, wrapped up unfortunately in religious terms. Others must have used her naivety to achieve their own objectives. And grandpa's Kikuyu customs that disconnected him from his babies at a time when they would have needed his personal care the most was not much help either. He ignorantly abandoned them to the care of strangers and several generations later his people have continued to suffer for the sins of their fathers. And behaviors of this kind have only retrogressed the peace and development of the world.

My relatives and I have led the life of victims during all our life. Our faith and customs blocked our ability to think. As opposed to confronting life issues, we so long ago resigned to scapegoats in place of action. We have felt helpless and in helplessness sent our issues, by way of prayers, to the cross of the risen Christ even when we did not have an adequate basis for that faith. I do not care whether our faith today is genuine or not. What angers me is the fact that I have every reason to believe a lot of my people do not have an adequate basis for it. They are not capable of explaining or living it and their lives are a contradiction of their professed faith. I know for sure that if people were able to delve deeper, they would realize the degree of harm that their belief system has caused them and their families over all these years. Where we preached prayers, I think, we should have been preaching love, humility, responsibility, common sense and hard work. Our individual way of thinking has had a significant influence on our villages, our children, our country, and we created monsters for our leaders. Instead of thinking about the future of our children, couples went ahead and populated the earth. My mother and her husband went ahead to have the eight of us and their action when multiplied by the birthing behavior of other parents has not done Africa any good. Why create problems and then pray to God for help to cure the maladies of our own creation?

My relatives, innocent as they may have always been, and I say this with tremendous respect, awe and honor for all the sacrifices that my parents made so that I could live, have continued to be negative forces that have contributed to the disrespect and humiliation the African has continued to suffer around the world. Why, if these black folks had realized that the white people were up to no good, for they had lived and been used by them; they had no hospitals, roads or schools that were meant for them after all the years the white people had ruled over them. And yet they continue to look up to the white people for help? It defies common sense. If I were white and you had chased me from your country and you continued to look up to me, why would I not take advantage of you? Why would I not think of you as a damn fool?

Africa should have been doing business with the west for centuries and any confused notion that the west will ever lift them from poverty is an illusion. It will never happen. Africa has many resources that the west desperately needs and all that is needed is Africa's recognition of her own value in order that she can competently negotiate with the world on her own terms. Africa needs to understand there are no free lunches and her people are being once again enslaved for she has failed to provide the opportunity to make them proud.

It does not matter that my relatives' intentions were innocent or good, for as they say, the road to hell is paved with good intentions. I blame us for inaction, for our naivety, for being frozen in time, for not questioning the basis of our way of life and for being scared of taking responsibility for events in our life. And this by the way is not about just my relatives. It is about all those mothers and fathers, sons and daughters who have drifted by and followed success around the world guided by childhood impressions of the world around us and what we understand that success to mean. I have watched with disgust the large numbers of immigrant families that come to Canada and in a few years get divorced when their childhood dreams are not fulfilled. For some strange chance, and I think God either loves me or my children and their mother for He has seen our innocence, we have managed to stick together.

Unlike the colonial governments before them, that used what they knew were the people's blind faith for religions that they hardly understood, African governments either ignored the potency of religion or when they saw its impact, they calculated it for their individual political advantage. They helped the people build bigger and bigger church halls, despite all the corruption, frustration and crime that were happening all around them. Kids went to school but then there were no jobs and everybody blamed everybody. Some people sought escape in foreign countries while others turned to crime. Yet others turned to the church and devoured God, feathers and all, as well as their fellow worshippers. Some became victims of prayers, sacrificing all they had at the many altars while others became villains of materialism, scooping away all that was brought to the altars for God. They were the new gods, who blessed and then consumed the seeds of success that had been planted by the rams.

I remember my experience the first time I went to study strategic management in the United Kingdom in 1993. The thing that struck me most was the people's

In The Thick of Things

outward approach to life. People enquired about business opportunities in Kenya and elsewhere in Africa, even when I thought their place was so good. I also remember the satisfaction that I felt when I quit my last employed job in Kenya. When I resolved to build my house in rural Kenya and how I felt when I saw the cassava plants sprout around my small *shamba*. I remember the joy I received the day my water well was completed and when those trees that I had planted around my patch of land sprouted. But then, we are all victims of our environments. I drifted away and followed 'success' overseas.

If I am able to forgive myself for drifting away from what I then knew to be good, perhaps I may also not have an adequate basis for blaming and not forgiving my mother and her contemporaries. I then have no business also of blaming the white people for colonizing Kenya and for preaching their religion. I think all I can do for now is to tell my story so that others can understand what it is that has gnawed my heart for so long in the hope that they too can learn and also be cured in the event that they were also hurting or were seeking an understanding of why the events around them have revolved the way they have. I think I can also do another thing; I can become more responsible, more active, more involved, more direct so that unlike my mother, somebody will not one day blame me for my inaction. I begin with my book.

I also think I have now finally been able to get out of this cocoon land. I think I am now cured of these maladies of ineptness and all. I now feel secure to project and surmise that in the event I was lucky enough to age to become a hundred years old, when for sure I shall be wanting to go away, for good, I think if anybody was to ask me then what to look out for in this world I would have the following to say to them: The world has two main kinds of people. On the one hand, there are those who create and use systems of men. On the other hand, you will find those that support and are used by the systems of men. In between and surrounding these two groups, you are going to find others who do not entirely fit into either of these two molds. They are described as rebels, chauvinists, outreach, wayward, rough diamonds, weird or with other words of a similar meaning.

Ahead of that time, I have come to the conclusion that one does not have to belong to the mainstream, because there is no mainstream. There are only people who use others and those that allow others to misuse them. You do not have to convince anybody of your right to belong because belonging is conventional. Conventional wisdom is unquestioning basic knowledge that is not necessarily true. There is no success or failure because life is just a journey. Good and evil need not be defined for us by anybody. For we all know what is good and what is evil. Even animals know what is good and what is evil. And this is the reason why they never harm their own children. For the standard of what is good or evil is always with us. When we do unto others what we would not want them to do unto us, what other measure do we need to know that we are hurting them?

We are the children of the universe. Just like the plants, the birds, the fish and the animals. And yet when we cut them down and use them we do not feel guilty, because some of our religions tell us that we have a superior right, even over their own lives. I believe we

In The Thick of Things

all have equal rights. Aim not to use or allow anybody to use you. Engage with respect, collaboratively and with consideration for the fulfillment of your life during your short period of being here. Do not hurt anybody and protect yourself and those that depend on you from being hurt and used by others.

There is no joy in having lots of the assets of the universe registered in your name. You do not need them. You will hardly ever use them. They belong to where you found them. Use all your talents, though, so that you may experience the joy of innovation and creativity, always being aware that what you discover becomes public goods that make the universe a better place. I think this is the difference between us and the rest of God's creation.

I have no quarrel with God and His creation, of which, I am a part. I have worshipped the God of Abraham, Jacob, Moses and Jesus Christ for over forty four years and my mother is a born again Christian. But I hate what is going on in Darfur, Iraq, Afghanistan, Somalia, Democratic Republic of the Congo and elsewhere. I have felt the pangs and pains of joblessness. I have been abused and ridiculed. I have also been with God's people, I mean church people, every Sunday for all these years. But I must give my piece. For, if it would ever happen, that we were to all finally go away before our stories were told, how will others know what they should expect? Of what value will our having been here be to us, and to them?

Should our God then be the same God of the Jews, the Muslims, the Hindus, Buddhists and the others? I would think the correct answer is yes. But do the faiths of these groups allow us to confidently share this view? I suspect they will not because they are suspicious of each other and they want to be different. Why would a bishop be led by a monk? And why should a Pope follow an Ayatollah? And it is as if these subtleties mattered.

In fact, even within the Christian faith, it has become important that one defines how they were baptized! Was it in the name of the Father, the Son and the Holy Spirit? Or was it by the sign of the cross, or by immersion in water? I am sure there is similar gobbledygook in all the other faiths and religions! To the extent that one would find these systems obstructive to the true religion of love and care I think it might even be in vain to want to belong to any of these folds.

The God I have been seeking out and the one I believe in is kind, generous, loving, selfless, does not condone injustice, does not partake in schemes aimed at exploiting other people, does not discriminate on the basis of material well-being, educational background, places of origin, skin color, language, religion, the food we eat, sex or body looks. And most of all He is not hypocritical. He is the God almighty. But where do you find the God almighty? Do you find him in a church, in a mosque, in a synagogue or where? Do you practice your faith like a Christian or like a Jew, like a Muslim or like a Hindu? I think it is possible to discard all these presentations and still be at peace with the almighty God. I think every human being is born with the capacity for doing both what is right and what is wrong. But we are blinded by conventional notions of success and failure, of good and evil to the extent that we mess our enjoyment of the resources of our planet, our dignity and our comfort and that of others as we try to be what it is not necessary for us to be. By the way, just so that you know, I have been to the Anglican Church where I was introduced as an infant, baptized, confirmed and became a born again Christian. I have also been to the church of Christ where I was baptized as an adult through emersion under water. I have also in recent years been to the Baptist church, the United church and back again to the Baptist church.

After all this involvement and searching, I now feel a deep sense of freedom. A new resolve, some kind of defiance, a new kind of assertiveness to do things in a slightly different way, and this has come at a period of apparent difficult circumstances. I think this has been a good time when people's raw attitudes towards you are less reserved. In any even what do they need from you in these circumstances?

I feel comfortable, like somebody with a new road map. I feel able to look ahead with confidence into the future without the baggage of the last forty-four years. I can categorically and authoritatively state that I believe I have some good answers for a number of the more difficult life issues and my place in this planet. I feel confident that I have gained some good experience and knowledge that should be shared with others in order that we may together make our world a better place.

Why for instance did my grandpa go out to the dances all the time when his mother expected him to have been working hard on the land to eke out an honest living? Did this have anything to do with the white people in Africa? Why did Jomo Kenyatta, Arap Moi and Kibaki and their age mates acquire so much land at the expense of poor Kenyans? How come the church that had become so entrenched in colonial Kenya never agitated for eradication of colonialism, the forceful grabbing of a nations wealth by foreigners? How come the western world has not supported and respected the people of Palestine following their democratic elections that put Hamas in power? How come we continue to do business with Libya and Saudi Arabia while at the same time insisting on democracy and the rule of law in Haiti, Zambia and Tanzania? How come Pakistan and General Musharaf are friends of the west? How come the youth soccer commentator could feel so comfortable to announce on TV that the young and hardworking Zambian boys that played excellent soccer in Burnaby, British Columbia were AIDS orphans and that they had not been to Canada before? How come he felt so comfortable to ridicule their Zambian coach on the basis of his physical looks despite all the good training he had given to these young boys who had kicked their way all through from Africa? Why have we been so relaxed with our attitudes and other people's attitudes towards us? What, for instance, would the Zambians lose if they were to deliberately decide they will never go play ball in places where they get abused?

At the end of the day, it is not about democracy. It is not about faith or religion. It is all about looking for practical and pragmatic solutions to the problems that we encounter in our lives. What makes a difference between successful society and a crumbling one is the ability to think creatively and to respect the fact that all human beings struggle with the same issues to several degrees. Our happiness does not come from having material possessions or living in certain countries. We achieve fulfillment though when we are able to stand up for whatever we believe in and give others respect while

In The Thick of Things

demanding that they respect our systems of thinking and doing things. We all have solutions to our problems and all that is needed is confidence that those around us are positive assets that we can team with to get the best out of our society.

Africa trusted about its inability to deal with its own issues and has looked up to others for so long for help and has ended up being thoroughly exploited and dehumanized. This will not change until that time her people finally own up to their problems and deal with their issues on their terms.

Chapter Eight

Conclusion

I think my objectives of writing this book have been achieved.

I hope the reader has acquired some different, hopefully positive perspective of viewing others. I have yearned to preach a message of true love in a unique way: a sincere way founded on pragmatic and real life experiences. If my treatise has come out this way, a key objective of my book has been accomplished. I believe that by giving the reader the opportunity to review my relatives' resumes, the factors that have shaped my perspectives would not only be understood and found genuine but might cause that reader to ponder and think. I hope I have managed to provoke the mind of the reader into a new awakening; a new way of thinking. If I have achieved this in whatever small way then I have finally achieved some degree of fulfillment. The journey that I have been through would therefore not be in vain for we learn from the experiences of others.

In The Thick of Things

We cherish William Wilberforce and his colleagues for bringing about the end of slave trade five hundred years ago. We also celebrate Dr. Martin Luther King Junior in recent years for his admonishment of white society in the United States to change their ways. We celebrate Rosa Parks and Nelson Mandela for their sacrifice and for standing up against injustice. I dare not compare my journey with that of these mighty heroes. But unless we share our small experiences with others, who knows who will gain from what experience?

It is poignant that we continue to do what we must to challenge our society which continues to entertain the same evils that we know belong to the past. We seem to be happy to pretend that all is good, even when we know this is not the case. We have behaved in the same way just as they did in those days. Some of us have been hurt and have walked into job search offices where officials made us feel guilty for having been dumped. There has to be something wrong with you, some appear to be saying when they seek my explanation regarding previous assignments.

What has continued to play out in my mind is the number of women, girls and boys who may have been raped but kept their silence so that they did not suffer the stigma of public scorn. And yet it is them who have been wronged! Is it the fault of those who hurt them that their pain remains bottled up? As I would advise them, I refuse to be stopped and I will shout at the pinnacles of the tallest buildings and from the top of the peaks of mountains until the noise becomes too much for the comfort of those who hurt my grandpa, my grandma, my parents and now me for I do not want my grandchildren to go down the same path that their relative victims trod before them. I will have failed them and I refuse to do that again! I refuse to feel helpless as my relatives did for I know each one of us has the power to make our world a better place for us all.

By reading my book and sharing its contents you help in a joint effort to make our world a better place for me, for you and for our posterity.

Thank you.

About the Author

The writer was born and lived in Africa for forty years where he overcame significant challenges in life.

His great grandparents lived through and survived the era of slave trade. His grandparents and his parents survived colonialism.

The author, while born "free", has been a cancer survivor for many years. In addition, he endured poverty, survived through the effects of trial and error systems of a new government in Africa before finally deciding to heed God's instructions to Adam - that we go out yonder and occupy the earth. He immigrated to North America, specifically Canada, where it turned out, upon arrival, that he was now a national of a colony of the British who once colonized his relatives before they agitated and gained their "freedom" long before the writer was born.

Despite being highly qualified in his field, he quickly became disillusioned when he got confronted with the realities of a prejudiced society. Instead of giving up hope he has persisted and continued to do what he believes is positive including pursuing more professional studies at his local community college.

He is married with two grown up children.

Printed in the United States
94238LV00001B/148-228/A